Becoming a Reflective Mathematics Teacher

A Guide for Observations and Self-Assessment

STUDIES IN MATHEMATICAL THINKING AND LEARNING
Alan H. Schoenfeld, Series Editor

Becoming a Reflective Mathematics Teacher

A Guide for Observations and Self-Assessment

Alice F. Artzt
Eleanor Armour-Thomas

Queens College of the City University of New York

LEA

LAWRENCE ERLBAUM ASSOCIATES, PUBLISHERS

2002   Mahwah, New Jersey   London

Lawrence Erlbaum Associates, Inc., Publishers
10 Industrial Avenue
Mahwah, NJ 07430

Cover design by Kathryn Houghtaling Lacey

Library of Congress Cataloging-in-Publication Data

Artzt, Alice F.
   Becoming a reflective mathematics teacher: a guide for observations and
self-assessment/ Alice F. Artzt, Eleanor Armour-Thomas
      p.   cm.
   Includes bibliographical references and indexes.
   ISBN 0-8058-3036-7 (cloth: alk. paper)—ISBN 0-8058-3037-5 (pbk.: alk. paper)
   1. Mathematics—Study and teaching—Evaluation. 2. Mathematics
teachers—Psychology. I. Armour-Thomas, Eleanor. II. Title.

QA11 .A784 2001
510'.71—dc21   00-067727

Books published by Lawrence Erlbaum Associates are printed on acid-free paper, and their bindings
are chosen for strength and durability.

Printed in the United States of America
10   9   8   7   6   5   4   3

This book is dedicated to our immediate families and our family of students.

Contents in Brief

Contents

List of Tables and Figures

Tables

Figures

Preface

Congratulations on your decision to become a mathematics teacher—a profession suited for a very select group of people. But keep in mind that great teachers are not born, they are made. Just as the most talented musicians or artists become great by reflecting on their art, beginning teachers become accomplished teachers, and skilled teachers become great teachers, by thinking hard about their teaching and finding ways to improve it. This book, based on over 20 years of research and teaching, will prepare you for your work in the mathematics classroom, and for developing the thoughtfulness and reflectiveness you need to become a great teacher.

A few obvious prerequisites are that you must be a good mathematician and a lover of mathematics. You must enjoy relating to young people and recognize the importance of their learning mathematics well. A less obvious prerequisite is your willingness and ability to be a reflective, self-critical thinker. As any experienced mathematics teacher will affirm, there is no such thing as a perfect lesson. There is always room for improvement. But whether you improve, or how well or how quickly you improve, depends on what you reflect on and assess before, during, and after your instructional practice. The key to developing into the type of mathematics teacher who can empower students with the love and understanding of mathematics is to continually question your teaching in ways that lead to sustainable changes in both your thinking and your classroom practice. This process of reflection and self-assessment must be approached in a knowledgeable and systematic way. Toward this end, we have created activities based on a model grounded in a cognitive perspective of student-centered teaching.

Part I provides background, giving you the "big picture" regarding mathematics teaching. In Chapter 1, you will learn about student-centered teaching—an approach to teaching that focuses not on flashy presentations but on what really counts: what your students come to understand and how you help them learn. There's more to teaching than meets the eye, and we will help you understand what it means to teach effectively. Chapter 2 takes a closer look at the image of teaching and learning discussed in Chapter 1 and describes a framework for examining the teaching process. That framework looks at two aspects of a lesson: phases and dimensions. In Chapter 3, we delve beneath the surface to find out what makes the classroom work. It is what the teacher knows and thinks that shapes what happens in the classroom. We'll present a framework for examining teacher cognitions and discuss the ways that those cognitions shape what the teacher does. Understanding this framework will help you make sense of lessons you see other people teach. And, more importantly, it will help you think about your own teaching. Before you learn how to use the frameworks presented in Chapters 2 and 3, you have a right to ask, "Does this approach make sense?" Chapter 4 shows that it does. We report on the research we have on the relationship between classroom teaching and teachers' underlying cognitions. After documenting the validity of the model and thus rounding out the theoretical frame, we are ready to turn to the "how to."

In Part II, we'll show you how to use the model to observe other teachers' classroom work, and then to use it to reflect on your own teaching. In Chapter 5, we give you detailed guidelines and instruments to use when observing other teachers' lessons. There are so many things to watch when observing someone else's classroom that if you are not focused, you will gain little from the experience. The techniques suggested in this chapter ensure that you will learn something different and worthwhile from each lesson you observe. The techniques you learned in Chapter 5 prepare you for the most important observations you will do in your career as a mathematics teacher—your observations of yourself. Chapter 6, possibly the most important chapter in the book, presents a detailed process for objectively examining both your own teaching of mathematics and your goals, knowledge, and beliefs that underlie everything you do in your classroom. You will learn how to prepare for lesson observations and postlesson conferences with your cooperating teacher or college supervisor in ways that will help them better understand your teaching. You want to be sure that during your postlesson conference, you share all that you thought about and learned from having taught the lesson. In this chapter, we give you specific techniques to help you analyze your lessons and your related thoughts in a detailed and comprehensive manner. Videotaping yourself and having your peers observe you can also be powerful tools for self-improvement, especially when done in the structured manner we discuss in this chapter. Finally in Chapter 6, we explain the value of expressing your thoughts and feelings in a written journal. We show you how rethinking the decisions you make during the course of instruction can help you improve your teaching. By examining your own and others' teaching in the way we have outlined in Part II, you have produced much written evidence of your growth as a teacher. In Chapter 7, we show you how you can organize these materials into a portfolio that will document your growth as a teacher. This portfolio can be used as part of the requirements for National Board Certification.

If you are still wondering whether or how the model works, you will want to read the case studies that we have included in Part III. You will see how we used the method to help five of our student teachers improve specific aspects of their instruction. Finally, in our conclusion, we summarize our feelings about and experiences with the model as well as the reactions of our student teachers.

Throughout the text, you will see examples of the work of our student teachers. Additionally, you can find the forms you need to apply the model in Appendixes B, C, and D. Please note that we used fictional names for all our students.

A NOTE TO PROFESSORS

This book can be used in various ways. The authors and others have used it as a secondary text for a mathematics teaching methods course. The structured observation activities are designed to help students relate the concepts they learn in their methods course to the instructional practice they observe in actual mathematics classrooms. This book has also been used to support the activities preservice teachers engage in as they student teach. The reflective activities provide a structure through which beginning teachers can think about their teaching in an insightful, thorough, and productive manner.

Students can work through the activities described in this book over the period of a year. The structured observations and reflective activities are modular, and the model applies to all observations of teaching, no matter what the instructional context. Thus the ideas and activities in this book can be of value when used as a supplement to a course that is already in place.

ACKNOWLEDGMENTS

Behind every book is a cast of characters making a unique and essential contribution. Our cast ranges from supportive family members, to hard working students, to encouraging colleagues, to wise and insightful experts in the field. While it is impossible to mention all of the people who directly or indirectly contributed to this book, we will do our best to mention the main cast and the roles that they played.

The book originated with the time-consuming work we did with our students. Our devoted husbands, Russ and Bernard, and our loving children Michele, Kurt, Julie, and Greg, and Renate and Bianca were understanding, encouraging, and supportive of the time we gave to these students and to the writing of the book. Our dear students who worked so hard to become the best mathematics teachers they could be played the starring roles. Several students deserve special mention as they contributed to this book in major ways: Sara Lamm helped do the videotaping and coding for the research project. Cindy Phillips, Alison Wank, and Dahlia Sacks wrote many of the insightful observation reports, self-reflective comments, and journal and portfolio entries included in the book.

The original model could not have taken form without feedback from many people. Carol Tittle and the late Zita Cantwell were our mentors in the early stages of the research. We will always be indebted to them for the endless hours they spent in advising us. The precurser to the teaching model presented here was a cognitive-metacognitive framework that we developed to examine problem solving in small groups. That framework was based on earlier ones designed by George Polya, Frank Lester, Joe Garofalo, and Alan Schoenfeld. The specific input given to us by Frank Lester and Alan Schoenfeld regarding the development of that framework was invaluable. It set the stage for how we would later consider teaching as problem solving.

When the first research reports were written, Elizabeth Fennema lent us her support, confidence, and advice. She was the first to plant the idea of turning our ideas and experiences into a book. Frank Lester later gave generously of his time and expertise in helping us shape the research articles for publication. Having his vote of confidence was what we needed to continue our efforts in this work.

Implementation of the model was made possible through the tireless efforts of Naomi Weinman. Not only did she work with the students but she helped shape the final versions of the activities used for self-reflection. She also spent endless hours identifying the most exemplary pieces of student work for inclusion in the book. Her role in this book cannot be overestimated. And thanks go to our dear friend and colleague Frances Curcio who lent us her support by using the model with her students and providing us feedback as well as her vote of confidence. She was the one who gave us the idea to submit our proposal for this book to Alan Schoenfeld's editorial series.

We also express our deepest appreciation to Naomi Silverman, Senior Editor at Lawrence Erlbaum Associates, for her encouragement, wise advice, and patience. We are indebted to both her and Lori Hawver, Assistant Editor, for their editorial expertise. Our gratitude extends to Sandra K. Wilcox, Michigan State University, and Mary Lynn Raith, Pittsburgh Public Schools, for their painstaking efforts in reviewing the manuscript for this book. Other thanks go to the Production Editor, Barbara Wieghaus, the Cover Designer, Kathryn Houghtaling Lacey, and the Production Manager, Lesley Rock, for their high quality and prompt work in putting the manuscript into its finished form.

Finally, thanks go to Alan Schoenfeld. From our beginning work on problem solving in small groups to the present work, he has given generously of his time, his wisdom, and his hands-on help. We feel comfortable in saying that through our entire research career in this area, he has been our main guiding light. When we presented this new work to him, Alan had the vision to turn this document into a "user-friendly" book. His editorial flair is evident throughout the pages of this book, so if it manages to contribute to the improvement of mathematics education, the main credit goes to him.

We are privileged to have stood on the shoulders of so many giants!

—*Alice F. Artzt*
—*Eleanor Armour-Thomas*

Part I

PHILOSOPHICAL BASIS FOR THE MODEL

Chapter 1

Toward an Understanding of Student-Centered Teaching

You have decided to become a mathematics teacher at a time when there is much excitement about reform in the mathematics education and research community. To reform means to do things differently. Expectations of teachers for the 21st century are very different from what they were as little as a generation ago. The purpose of this chapter is to give you a vision of what reform teaching looks like and the issues you must consider to teach that way.

INSTRUCTIONAL PRACTICE IN MATHEMATICS

What does it mean to be a competent mathematics teacher? What do you envision when you think of a good mathematics lesson? Picture two lessons involving probability. In the first lesson, the teacher presents a clear lecture providing all the definitions and rules. The students take copious notes and then, after watching the teacher model how to do a few problems, they do some practice problems at their seats. The teacher then brings the class together and answers questions about how to do the problems. In the second lesson, the teacher engages the students in an unfair game of dice. The students must make conjectures regarding the fairness of the game. They work in pairs to figure out why the game is unfair and then have a class discussion in which they inadvertently construct the concepts of probability underlying the game. The teacher helps the students organize and formalize their ideas.

As you may have guessed, the reform movement supports the type of teaching exemplified in the second lesson. In contrast to the teacher of the first lesson, who dispenses information to passive students, the teacher of the second lesson provides an interesting problem to students actively engaged in the problem-solving process with one another. The teacher oversees, guides, and facilitates the students' construction of new knowledge. Endorsement for this latter type of teaching comes from the literature on how students learn mathematics. That is, research suggests that learning is an active problem-solving process in which social interaction plays a critical role (Cobb, 1986; Vygotsky, 1978). Learning is facilitated when learners are encouraged to link new information to their prior knowledge and thereby generate new understandings (Fennema, Carpenter, & Peterson, 1989; Greeno, 1989; Lampert, 1986; Noddings, 1990; Von Glasersfeld, 1987).

In line with this research, the Professional Standards for Teaching Mathematics (1991) and the most recent Principles and Standards for School Mathematics (2000) suggest that teachers must create opportunities that stimulate, guide, and encourage students to make connections among mathematics concepts, construct mathematical ideas, solve problems through reasoning, and take responsibility for their own learning.

TEACHING IS MORE THAN MEETS
THE EYE

Although it is true that a competent teacher must engage in classroom behaviors that are likely to promote student learning of mathematics, this is not the full story of professional competence. There is growing recognition that teaching involves more than what teachers actually do in the classroom and extends to the driving forces behind the teacher's actions: their cognitions. For example, if you were to interview the two teachers described in the previous section about their lessons, what differences would you expect to find? What issues do you think they would discuss? For example, which teacher would be more apt to focus on covering the content? Which teacher would be more apt to focus on student understanding?

Recently, researchers have begun to build frameworks and models that seek to understand the mind and related actions of a teacher (e.g., Artzt & Armour-Thomas, 1998; Fennema & Franke, 1992; Schoenfeld, 1998; Simon, 1997). Our conceptualization on this issue is that teacher knowledge, beliefs, and goals directly influence decision making across three stages of teaching: *preactive* (planning), *interactive* (monitoring and regulating), and *postactive* (evaluating and revising). These components form a network of overarching cognition that directs and controls the instructional behaviors of teachers in the classroom. To examine both areas of teaching (instructional practice and cognitions), we developed a model of two interrelated frameworks grounded in a student-centered perspective of teaching. The first framework, which we call the Phase-Dimension Framework (PDF), consists of indicators of instructional practice and is described in detail in Chapter 2. The other framework, the Teacher Cognition Framework (TCF), consists of indicators of teacher cognitions and is elaborated on in Chapter 3.

THE CHALLENGE OF FACILITATING STUDENT-CENTERED TEACHING

Although there is broad agreement in the mathematics education and research community concerning the cognitive view of learning and its implications for teaching, it is not yet well understood how to help teachers develop student-centered practices in the classroom and the cognitions that guide and shape such practices.

One difficulty is that not enough is yet known about how to change the deeply entrenched beliefs about mathematics learning and teaching that are based largely on our own experiences as students. For example, an unfortunate yet widely held belief about teaching is that the role of the teacher is to transmit mathematical content, demonstrate procedures for solving problems, and explain the process of solving sample problems. Another outdated yet commonly held belief about learning is that students learn the content by listening well to the teacher and remembering what they are told. In this narrow view, students show that learning has occurred by applying the demonstrated procedures and working problems similar to the ones introduced earlier by the teacher.

Another difficulty involves the unpredictability of change, even among teachers given the same learning experiences intended to transform their teaching. Predicting change can be inaccurate because each prospective teacher comes to a learning situation with an existing cognitive structure that includes certain personal beliefs, knowledge, and goals. Although a group of teachers might be exposed to the same learning experiences, what one teacher notices and acts on depends on how the experiences filter through his or her unique existing cognitive structure. Consequently, different interpretations of the same experiences could lead to differential patterns of change. In short, understanding new teachers' trajectories is still an inexact science.

Despite these difficulties, current cognitive models of teacher change maintain that teachers move through pathways that culminate in student-centered practice (e.g., Cooney, 1993; Cooney & Shealy, 1997; Fennema, Carpenter, Franke, Levi, Jacobs, & Empson, 1996; Franke, Fennema, & Carpenter, 1997). In reviewing these studies, Goldsmith and Schifter (1997) identified three stages of teaching. The *initial stage* is characterized by traditional instruction, where the teacher is driven by the belief that students learn best by receiving clear information transmitted by a knowledgeable teacher. In *subsequent stages* of instruction, the teacher is more focused on helping students build on what they understand and less focused on helping them in the sole acquisition of facts. The instruction is founded on the teacher's belief that students should take greater responsibility in their own learning. In what Goldsmith and Schifter call the *final stage,* instruction is in line with the reform movement recommendations. (We prefer to refer to this stage as an *advanced stage* of teaching to indicate that there is always potential for future growth.) At this advanced stage, the teacher arranges experiences for students in which they actively explore mathematical topics, learning both the hows and whys of mathematical concepts and processes. The teacher is motivated by the belief that, given appropriate settings, students are capable of constructing deep and connected mathematical understanding.

We address the question of teacher change in our mathematics education program by requiring prospective teachers to use a reflection and self-assessment procedure. We believe that if teachers are to become truly studented centered in their teaching, they must view themselves as agents in their own learning and development. They must be willing and able to take responsibility for their actions in the classroom by giving careful consideration to what they intend to do not only before and during the lesson but after the lesson as well. To recognize that one must be committed to thinking deeply about various aspects of one's teaching is to climb the first step on the ladder of change. More than 30 years ago, Dewey (1933) defined this type of thinking as reflective thinking: "The active, persistent and careful consideration of any belief or supposed form of knowledge in light of the grounds that support it" (p. 9).

Reflection, though necessary, is not sufficient for transformative teaching. Teachers must also be willing and able to *acknowledge* problems that may be revealed as a result of the reflective process. Moreover, they must explore the reasons for the acknowledged problem, consider more plausible alternatives, and eventually *change* their thinking and subsequent action in the classroom. We argue that over time, the habitual use of reflective and self-assessment processes about learning experiences leads to transformation in teaching.

DEFINITION OF REFLECTION
AND SELF-ASSESSMENT

Reflection is defined as thinking about teaching. It involves the thoughts teachers have before, during, and after the actual enactment of a lesson. Although there are many definitions of reflection (e.g., Dewey, 1933; Schon, 1983; Van Manen, 1977; Von Glasersfeld, 1991), the construct resembles several of the thinking processes identified by Polya (1945) in his conception of mathematical problem solving: understanding, planning, and looking back. In Polya's model of problem solving, expert problem solvers think about the problem to be solved by using thinking processes indicative of understanding and planning. We contend that teachers must engage in similar types of thinking before the actual enactment of a lesson. For example, they must think about their goals for the students and thereby activate their knowledge and beliefs about the students, pedagogy, and the content itself. Teachers also must think about the difficulties students are likely to encounter in their efforts to attain the goals; consequently, teachers must think about the strategies they will need to consider in conducting the anticipated lesson.

Continuing with the problem-solving analogy, we view Polya's "looking back" as another type of reflective thinking that teachers engage in after conducting a lesson. In other words, just as an expert problem solver reexamines the steps taken to solve a problem, a teacher, on completing a lesson, must rethink lesson goals and reconsider what the teacher and the students said, did, and felt during the lesson. This reflective phase is likely to uncover difficulties or problems that, if the teacher does not address, may impede progress toward self-improvement in teaching. How do teachers increase the likelihood that problematic aspects of their teaching are indeed revealed during this reflective process? And, as importantly, what conjectures or judgments do they make about such difficulties?

The second strand in our procedure is self-assessment. Self-assessment describes the kinds of evaluative questions teachers ask themselves as they reflect on their teaching after completing lessons.

Taking personal responsibility and control of one's learning is a hallmark of academic excellence. A critical factor in this type of learning that researchers define as self-regulated (e.g., Harris, 1979; Paris & Newman, 1990; Zimmerman, 1990) is self-assessment. When students are in the habit of asking themselves questions such as "What do I need to do?" "How am I doing?" and "How well did I do?" in relation to academic goals, their learning is more proficient than that of students who do not habitually ask themselves these questions. Indeed, most contemporary models of human cognition consider self-assessment an important dimension of good thinking (Brown, 1978; Flavell, 1981; Schoenfeld, 1987; Sternberg, 1986). Likewise, we believe that self-assessment plays a pivotal role in enabling teachers to become student centered. The focus of teachers' self assessment may be quite varied, ranging from prelesson thoughts, lesson plans, and classroom practices to specific pedagogical actions taken during the actual teaching of lessons.

In our teacher education program, we used procedures of reflection and self-assessment to enable preservice teachers to examine the relationship between their cognitions and instructional practice. Our integrative model of teaching (the PDF and TCF) provided the conceptual guidance for their reflections and self-assessment.

LEARNING EXPERIENCES FOR PROMOTING TEACHER GROWTH

As a prospective teacher, you need to engage in specific learning experiences that put you on the road to having a successful profession as a mathematics teacher. Specifically, you need to participate in structured activities that get you in the habit of reflecting on and assessing your cognitions and your instructional practice.

During the beginning of your teacher preparatory program, it is important to observe other mathematics teachers. This experience helps sensitize you to some of the major areas of teachers' work in the classroom. Structured observation assignments encourage you to make conjectures about the cognitions of the teachers you observe and to consider the role of cognition in teaching.

During your student teaching experiences, you should be provided with supervision that encourages you to engage in structured reflection and self-assessment that are based on the model described in this book. This guidance is based on Vygotsky's (1978) idea that certain kinds of assistance influence growth in thinking. The first type of assistance, which some researchers (Wood, Bruner, & Ross, 1976) call "scaffolding," is given when a knowledgeable adult or capable peer interacts with a novice learner. These individuals listen, prompt, ask questions, and give feedback, and in so doing give just the right amount of assistance to advance the learner's understanding. As the learner's understanding develops, the adult or capable peer gradually reduces instructional assistance and allows the learner to assume greater independence for his or her learning. The second type of assistance occurs when an individual uses tools to support thinking and learning. Goldsmith and Schifter (1997) give an example of writing as a tool for facilitating intellectual growth: "Writing allows us to stop, reflect, think, reflect again, and struggle to articulate further. Having a physical record of the thinking process also broadens the opportunities for sharing ideas and engaging in dialogue with a wide variety of others (as well as with self), thus expanding the possibilities for developing further understanding" (p.43).

By observing teachers in the field, you can begin to examine classroom practices and speculate about the cognitions that may undergird such classroom behavior. During student teaching, your supervisor, cooperating teacher, and peers perform the conceptual scaffolding function. Tools such as journal writing, videotaping, written comments about thoughts before and after the lesson, and portfolios can help you to reflect on and assess your cognitions and classroom practice. The integrative model (the PDF and TCF) provides the conceptual basis for your observations in the field and the scaffolding activities. And finally, the reflection and self-assessment procedure help you to gain a more insightful understanding of the relationship between your cognitions and instructional practice.

Chapter 2

A Framework
for the Examination
of Instructional Practice

In this chapter, we demonstrate how to dissect a lesson, looking at its pieces and how they fit together. This approach orients your examination of others' teaching and helps you focus on important aspects of your own lessons. The first decomposition of a lesson is temporal and straightforward; we describe the parts of a lesson as it unfolds. The second decomposition is more complex; we discuss lesson dimensions and dimension indicators—the material of the lesson and how to think about it.

One challenge facing teacher educators today is how to prepare their students to teach in a manner consistent with new ideas about learning and the nature of mathematics. In the previous chapter, we identified a number of propositions about student learning that suggest new roles and responsibilities for teachers. We have developed a Phase-Dimension Framework (PDF) to help teachers better understand and appreciate these roles and responsibilities from a new cognitive perspective that has student learning as its focus.

Teaching for student learning with understanding is at the heart of the framework. We believe it is the essence of student-centered teaching and provides focus and direction for teachers' energies in the classroom. Two issues guided us in this belief. First, with others in the mathematics research and education community, we share the view that a primary goal of instruction is to promote student learning of mathematics with understanding (Hiebert & Carpenter, 1992). Second, theoretical and empirical research on learning from psychology, mathematics education, and cognitive science suggests positive consequences for students who learn with understanding. For example, some researchers claim that initial understanding enables children to construct relationships and create productive inventions (Hiebert & Carpenter, 1992). Others have shown that learning with understanding promotes remembering (Bartlett, 1932; Rumelhart, 1975) and enhances transfer (Brown, Collins, & Duguid, 1989; Perkins & Salomon, 1989).

What would classroom practice look like if the goal of teaching were to enable student learning of mathematics with understanding? More specifically, how would teachers help students to relate new ideas of mathematics to what they already know and can do, use their prior knowledge and skill to construct new meaning through reasoning and problem solving, and extend their learning to new contexts? We created two classifications to answer these questions: lesson phases and lesson dimensions.

LESSON PHASES

Lesson phases describe a temporal sequence of teaching-learning experiences that occur over the duration of a lesson. The concept of lesson phases is derived from the cognitive instruction literature that suggests that the ways teachers initiate, develop, and close instructional episodes have important implications for student learning (e.g., Jones, Palincsar, Ogle, & Carr, 1987). Lesson phases function as transition markers that indicate different segments of an enacted lesson. For example, when designing instruction, teachers must ensure that they set aside time in which they (a) establish students' readiness for learning, (b) build new concepts by enabling learners to recognize relationships and construct new meanings, and (c) enable learners to integrate and extend their learning to new contexts. It is important to note that, although each of these phases is essential for effective instruction, they need not all occur in one class period. For example, an interesting problem might have different components that the class needs to work on for several days before the main ideas are developed. However, for the purpose of clarity, it is helpful to students for the teacher to identify the specific phase of instruction in which they are engaged. For example, before a summarizing activity takes place, the teacher might make it clear to the students that it is now time to tie up all the ideas that they have learned thus far.

We adopted the descriptors for these temporal phases of a lesson from the Connecticut Competency Instrument for Beginning Teachers: initiation, development and closure. (For further discussion of the use of these terms, see Armour-Thomas & Szczesiul, 1989.)

LESSON DIMENSIONS

Table 1 provides a bird's eye view of a lesson, focusing on its most important dimensions. The major categories described in Table 1—tasks, learning environment, and discourse—are fundamental components of a lesson. In this section, we describe the characteristics of each component and explore how they work.

Tasks

Tasks provide opportunities for learners to connect their knowledge to new information and to build on their knowledge and interest through active engagement in meaningful problem solving. According to the general literature, to foster student involvement, tasks must be motivational, at an appropriate level of difficulty, and sequenced in a meaningful way so that different representations are available to help students clarify and connect their ideas. A further elaboration of these ideas follows.

Modes of Representation

Modes of representation are the forms for representing mathematical concepts or principles externally through the use of verbal or written words, diagrams, manipulatives, computers, or calculators. Research suggests that how individuals represent information in memory is partly influenced by the form of the content represented (Brown & Baird, 1993; Hiebert & Carpenter, 1992). In creating opportunities for children to learn with understanding, teachers must figure out what modes of representing mathematics concepts and principles are likely to help them make connections with these ideas.

Motivation

Motivation is a key concept in learning. According to Good and Brophy (1995) "motivation is a hypothetical construct used to explain the initiation, direction, intensity, and persistence of goal-directed behavior"

TABLE 1
Lesson Dimensions and Dimension Indicators

Dimensions	*Description of Dimension Indicators*
Tasks	
Modes of representation	Uses such representations as symbols, diagrams, manipulatives, computer or calculator representations accurately to facilitate content clarity. Provides multiple representations that enable students to connect their prior knowledge and skills to the new mathematical situation.
Motivational strategies	Uses tasks that capture students' curiosity and inspires them to speculate and to pursue their conjectures. Takes into account the diversity of student interests and experiences. The substance of the motivation is aligned with the goals and purposes of instruction
Sequencing and difficulty levels	Sequences tasks so that students can progress in their cumulative understanding of a particular content area and can make connections between ideas learned in the past and those they will learn in the future. Uses tasks that are suitable to what the students already know and can do and what they need to learn or improve on.
Learning environment	
Social and intellectual climate	Establishes and maintains a positive rapport with and among students by showing respect for and valuing students' ideas and ways of thinking. Enforces classroom rules and procedures to ensure appropriate classroom behavior.
Modes of instruction and pacing	Uses instructional strategies that encourage and support student involvement as well as facilitate goal attainment. Provides and structures the time necessary for students to express themselves and explore mathematical ideas and problems.
Administrative routines	Uses effective procedures for organization and management of the classroom so that time is maximized for students' active involvement in the discourse and tasks.
Discourse	
Teacher-student interaction	Communicates with students in a nonjudgmental manner and encourages the participation of each student. Requires students to give full explanations and justifications or demonstrations orally and/or in writing. Listens carefully to students' ideas and makes appropriate decisions regarding when to offer information, provide clarification, model, lead, and let students grapple with difficulties.
Student-student interaction	Encourages students to listen to, respond to, and question each other so that they can evaluate and, if necessary, discard or revise ideas and take full responsibility for arriving at mathematical conjectures and/or conclusions.
Questioning	Poses variety of levels and types of questions using appropriate wait times that elicit, engage, and challenge students' thinking.

Note. From "A Cognitive Model for Examining Teachers' Instructional Practice in Mathematics: A Guide for Facilitating Teacher Reflection," by A. F. Artzt and E. Armour-Thomas, 1999, *Educational Studies in Mathematics, 40*(3), p. 217. Copyright © 1999 by Kluwer Academic Publishers. Adapted with kind permission from Kluwer Academic Publishers.

(p. 343). This means that the tasks that students engage in must possess attributes that attract and sustain their attention and emotional investment over time. In applying this construct to mathematical tasks, teachers must consider three basic questions:

- Are the tasks in alignment with the lesson goal of learning with under-standing?
- Will the tasks arouse students' curiosity and interest and inspire them to speculate and pursue conjectures?
- Will the tasks be sufficiently challenging to sustain students' interest until completion?

Difficulty Level and Sequencing

The level of difficulty of a task is its complexity, and sequencing is the order in which students attend to and work on features of the task and/or the order in which the teacher makes the task salient for them. Teachers must decide how and when to sequence tasks and how to select tasks with appropriate levels of difficulty. If a task is too easy, students will lose interest, become bored, and apply minimal effort. Conversely, if the tasks are so difficult that students cannot succeed, many will become frustrated and give up trying. Therefore, the difficulty level and sequencing of a task must allow students to use their past knowledge and experience to help them understand the requirements of the task. Yet, the task must be chal-lenging enough that students create new connections to deepen their understanding and extend their learning. These attributes of tasks are con-sistent with the suggestion of the National Council of Teachers of Mathe-matics (NCTM, 1991) that tasks must "engage all students in formulating and solving a wide variety of problems, making conjectures and con-structing arguments, validating solutions, and evaluating the reasonable-ness of mathematical claims" (p. 21).

Learning Environment

The term *learning environment* describes the conditions under which the teaching-learning process unfolds in the classroom. It defines the tone and patterns of interpersonal interactions between student and teacher as well as the terms for such engagement. It also refers to the circumstances that affect the flow of action in the classroom and the mechanisms by which time is allocated for learning. This definition of *learning environment* is similar to the concept of *context* as it has been used in the educational and psychological literature for many years. For example, some researchers assert that the context in which cognitive activity is undertaken shapes not only the perceived nature of the problem but the solution as well (Rogoff & Lave, 1984; Vygotsky, 1978). The psychological significance of the context is consistent with NCTM's (1991) vision of a learning environment as one that promotes the development of students' conceptual and procedural understanding.

In making decisions about learning environments, teachers can consider several categories of attributes. The first category, and perhaps the one most directly related to the promotion of student learning with understanding, has to do with the social and intellectual climate of the classroom. The question is whether the environment is conducive to the discourse and task engagement likely to foster the development of mathematical understanding among all students. The second category of attributes concerns the modes of instruction and amount of class time allotted for them. The third concern has to do with practical or technical issues related to classroom organization and management, such as the classroom furniture arrangement, routines, rules for student deportment, and allocation of time for administrative activities. A further elaboration of these attributes follows.

Social and Intellectual Climate

The social and intellectual climate defines the tone, style, and manner of the interpersonal interactions in the classroom. Research in the humanistic tradition (Bossert, 1977; Rogers, 1983) has emphasized the importance of affective and emotional elements in interpersonal relationships and their implications for student social and cognitive growth and development. When the interpersonal chemistry in a classroom is positive, students are encouraged to activate and use their prior knowledge in relation to the problem at hand and to engage in the process of knowledge consolidation and construction. When the social and intellectual climate is positive, it supports a feeling of mutual respect among and between students and teacher, and all have patience for one another and value diverse ideas and ways of thinking. It creates a safe haven for students to engage in challenging tasks without the fear of failure or threat of punishment.

Modes of Instruction and Pacing

Modes of instruction are the activities that teachers use in the classroom to help students attain the objectives of the lesson. Activities include seatwork, discussions, recitation, pair work, lab work, guided discovery, and small-group work, to name a few. To facilitate student learning with understanding, instructional activities must encourage students' active exploration of mathematical ideas and stimulate their thinking in ways that build and deepen mathematical understanding. Moreover, teachers must properly pace activities so that students are provided enough time in which to express themselves freely, make and test conjectures, debate ideas with one another, and construct new knowledge.

Administrative Routines

Administrative routines are predictable or ritualized procedures or activities in classroom organization and management. Saphier and Gower (1987) identify three types of routines of importance in the classroom: those that are concerned with housekeeping (e.g., distribution of materials and equipment, attendance, and cleanup); routines related to class business (e.g., taking turns, collecting homework); and those that pertain to work procedures (e.g., use of equipment and tools, and procedures for doing assignments). Kounin and Gump (1974) assert that routines provide an on-going signal of organizational and interpersonal behavior in the classroom. The less time teachers spend on these technical administrative aspects of the learning environment, the more time they have for engaging students in activities more directly related to learning mathematics with understanding.

Discourse

Discourse describes the verbal exchange among members of the community in the classroom, both teachers and students. Discourse can facilitate task engagement for learning with understanding. There are many critical features of discourse that define the nature and quality of interactions among members: the kinds of questions posed, the responses elicited, and time allowed for responding. Let us examine these attributes of discourse further.

Teacher-Student Interactions

Some researchers studying mathematics from a constructivist perspective call attention to the importance of social relationships in teaching. They conceive of the classroom as a potential learning community in which students experience a sense of efficacy as learners and thus show a willingness to take risks for learning in a public forum (Richards, 1991; Wood, Cobb, & Yackel, 1995). This means that teachers should interact as mathematical learners on an equal basis with students, always in search of more in-depth mathematical understanding and discovery. Through questions, comments, and feedback, the teacher may press the students to reflect on what they or their classmates have asked or proposed to build and extend their own understandings. Furthermore, the teacher may encourage students to attend to and stay engaged in the task at hand and solicit contributions from everyone. The teacher plays a critical role in orchestrating discourse. According to the *Professional Standards for Teaching Mathematics* (NCTM, 1991), teachers must think very carefully about "when to provide information, when to clarify an issue, when to model, when to lead, and when to let a student struggle with a difficulty" (p. 35).

Student-Student Interactions

For students to build their own mathematical constructions, they need to interact with each other in ways that reinforce and support yet challenge each others' ideas. Within the classroom environment as a community of learners, students should be encouraged to listen to, respond to, and question each other; to debate and give explanations and justifications for their ideas and feedback to their peers' ideas. The nature and quality of these student-student interactions, though, must encourage students to make connections of their prior knowledge to new information, to make new connections between mathematical ideas, and to integrate and extend these new understandings into their existing knowledge structures.

Questioning

Questioning in teacher-student interaction is an important medium through which students build on their preexisting knowledge. The level and type of questioning as well as the time for student responses vary in the classroom because this medium serves many purposes. Research shows that both the cognitive level of questions (Klinzing, Klinzing-Eurich, & Tisher, 1985; Samson, Strykowski, Weinstein, & Walberg, 1987) and time for responding to teacher questions (Rowe, 1986; Tobin, 1983) have had positive consequences for students in terms of their quality of participation and achievement. Through questioning, the teacher encourages students to make public their knowledge, skills, and attitudes in relation to the problem under consideration. Teacher questioning may also seek to determine how well students are making connections or the kinds of connections that are being made among mathematical ideas. Confrey (1990) suggests that the following types of questions promote student learning with understanding: What are we doing? What is the problem? What does this problem say? Why? What does that tell you? What can you tell me? Why not? What do you mean it doesn't work?" (p. 116). Depending on the cognitive demands of the questions and the student's level of understanding, the teacher determines how much time to allow for student responses. When students respond to the questions, the teacher may decide to adjust the pace of teaching, reteach, or reinforce the concepts. The *Professional Standards for Teaching Mathematics* (NCTM, 1991) acknowledges the critical role of teacher questioning and suggests that the teacher's role begins to shift from telling and describing to listening, questioning, and probing for understanding.

In our work with teachers, we have found that these attributes have allowed us to better understand variation among instructional practice. The next chapter describes the framework we used to examine the cognitions underlying these areas of instructional practice.

Chapter 3

A Framework
for the Examination
of Teacher Cognitions

In this chapter, we show you how to examine the aspects of teaching that are the driving force behind every lesson: teacher cognitions. This approach allows you to better understand your own and others' teaching, and provides the mechanism with which you can engage in self-reflection and improvement. As we have argued, what counts is the teachers' cognition and how it comes into play at different times. Table 2 provides an overview of the nature of teacher cognition and when it gets applied. The overarching aspects of teacher cognition are teachers' *goals, knowledge,* and *beliefs.* Other cognitions come into play at different times and in different ways: planning prior to the lesson, monitoring and regulating during the lesson, and evaluating and revising after the lesson.

Student-centered instruction must be backed by mental activities and thought processes of teachers who have a student-centered philosophy of instruction. Based on our position that teacher cognitions drive teachers' actions in the classroom, we developed a Teacher Cognitions Framework (TCF), using the same conceptual orientation as the Phase-Dimension Framework (PDF): teaching for student learning with understanding. We used Jackson's (1968) conceptual distinction of preactive, interactive, and postactive stages of teaching to examine teacher cognitions before, during, and after teaching a lesson. We identified two broad components of cognition: overarching cognitions and cognitive processes. A brief

TABLE 2
Components of Teacher Cognitions and Description of Indicators

Cognitions	Description of Indicators of Cognition
Overarching Conditions	
Goals	Desires to help students construct their own meaning so that they will develop conceptual as well as procedural understanding and will value mathematics and feel confident in their abilities.
Knowledge	
Pupils	Has specific knowledge of pupils' prior knowledge and experiences, abilities, attitudes, and interests.
Content	Has conceptual and procedural understandings of the content and is aware of and appreciates the connections between it and past and future areas of study.
Pedagogy	Understands how students learn mathematics and knows how to develop suitable teaching strategies and anticipate and prepare for areas of difficulty based on that understanding.
Beliefs	
Pupils	Views the role of students as active participants in their own learning. Believes students should make conjectures, propose approaches and solutions to problems, debate the validity of one another's claims, and verify, revise, and discard ideas on the basis of their own and other students' mathematical reasoning.
Content	Views mathematics as a "dynamic and expanding system of connected principles and ideas constructed through exploration and investigation" (NCTM, 1991, p. 133).
Pedagogy	Views the teacher's role as a facilitator of student learning through selections of problem-solving tasks and the leading and orchestration of communication in which students are challenged to think for themselves through mathematical reasoning.
Cognitive Processes	
Preactive	
Planning	Focuses lesson on building conceptual understanding based on what the students already know, and focuses on mathematical processes underlying the procedures to be developed as well as the skill development required by the content specifications. Sequences tasks logically to build on previous student understanding and to clarify new concepts and arouse students' interest and curiosity. Makes obvious how much time is allowed for each segment of the lesson (initiation, development, closure).
Interactive	
Monitoring	Observes, listens to, and elicits participation of students on an ongoing basis to assess student learning and disposition toward mathematics.
Regulating	Adapts or changes plans while teaching based on the information received through monitoring student learning and interest.
Postactive	
Evaluating	Describes and comments on students' understanding of concepts and procedures and dispositions toward mathematics as well as the effects of instruction on these outcomes.
Revising	Uses information from evaluations of student learning and instructional practices to revise and adapt subsequent plans for instruction.

description of these aspects of teachers' mental activities follows, along with examples of their potential impact on the dimensions of instructional practice discussed in Chapter 2: tasks, learning environment, and discourse.

OVERARCHING COGNITIONS

There are three components of overarching cognitions: goals, knowledge, and beliefs. The centrality of these components to teaching is supported by extensive research (e.g., Schoenfeld, 1998). We use the term *overarching* because we think that these cognitions comprise a dynamic network that functions as a control center for all our thoughts and actions about teaching. It is these overarching cognitions that influence the decisions teachers make before (*planning*), during (*monitoring* and *regulating*) and after (*evaluating* and *revising*) a lesson.

Goals

We define *goals* as expectations about the intellectual, social, and emotional outcomes for students as a consequence of their classroom experiences. In the *Curriculum and Evaluation Standards for School Mathematics,* the NCTM (1989) sets forth its vision of mathematical power through the articulation of five general goals for all students: that they value mathematics, become confident in their ability to do mathematics, become mathematical problem solvers, learn to communicate mathematically, and learn to reason mathematically (p. 5). More recently, in their *Principles and Standards for School Mathematics,* the NCTM (2000) reiterated the importance of these processes and expressed their expectation that teachers reflect these goals in their instructional practice. Furthermore, researchers (Hiebert, 1986; Silver, 1986) as well as recent reform initiatives (MSEB & NRC, 1991) have begun to give more attention to goals that emphasize the importance of teaching for conceptual as well as procedural understanding.

Teachers' goals (often implicit) become apparent through observations of their instructional practices. For example, a teacher whose goal is that students learn to value mathematics tends to design meaningful and worthwhile tasks. A teacher whose goal is to have students communicate mathematically tends to include such instructional routines as small-group work that facilitates such communication. Finally, a teacher whose goal is that students engage in mathematical reasoning tends to orchestrate the classroom discourse in such a way that the burden of explanation and justification is placed on the students.

Knowledge

We define teacher knowledge as an integrated system of internalized information acquired over time about pupils, content, and pedagogy. This definition is based in part on Shulman's (1986) conception of teacher knowledge as a multidimensional and interrelated construct that includes content knowledge, pedagogical content knowledge, and curricular knowledge. More recently, other researchers have concurred that these categories of knowledge are important for teaching (Ball, 1990; Borko & Putman, 1996; Brown & Borko, 1992; Schoenfeld, 1998) and can make a difference in instructional practice and student learning (Fennema & Franke, 1992; Peterson, 1988).

Although it is not yet clear how these categories of knowledge are organized and structured in memory in ways to inform lesson planning and classroom practice, we do know that teacher knowledge reveals itself in different ways throughout classroom instruction. For example, in our exploratory study we found that teachers who seemed to know their students well (their prior knowledge and experiences, their interests and attitudes, and their learning styles and abilities) created tasks that were motivational and at an appropriate level of difficulty. Teachers who seemed to have a broad knowledge of pedagogical approaches and knew how these approaches fit the needs of different students and different content areas tended to use a wide range of instructional strategies that could enhance the learning opportunities for their students. Teachers who seemed to have a deep knowledge of the content and were aware of and appreciated its connections with past and future areas of study tended to ask a variety of questions of different levels that focused on both procedural and conceptual issues. The type of questions they asked helped students make the connections necessary for them to construct new understandings.

Beliefs

We define beliefs as an integrated system of personalized assumptions about the nature of the subject, the students, learning, and teaching. Beliefs function as an interpretative filter for teachers' goals and knowledge that strongly impact classroom practice (Cooney, 1985; Ernest, 1989; Schoenfeld, 1998; Swafford, 1995; Thompson, 1992). For example, to provide classroom opportunities for students to understand mathematics as a "dynamic and expanding system of connected principles and ideas constructed through exploration and investigation" (NCTM, 1991, p.133) teachers must believe it is such. Only then can they design tasks that provide opportunities for students to act like real mathematicians who engage in authentic mathematical inquiry. Furthermore, teachers who consider themselves facilitators of student learning tend to use instructional strategies that foster communication among students and challenge students to think for themselves and engage in mathematical reasoning. Finally, teachers who believe that the role of *all* students in the classroom is to be active participants in their own learning tend to create social and intellectual climates that set the stage for discourse that can offer every student an equal opportunity to participate.

Although beliefs are undoubtedly a driving force behind the nature of a teacher's instructional practice, teachers' stated beliefs are not always consistent with their behavior. In our own research on this issue (Artzt & Armour-Thomas, 1998), we found that several teachers professed beliefs about how to teach mathematics consistent with ideas espoused by the NCTM (1989), yet their classroom practice suggested otherwise. A possible reason for this may have to do with the readiness of the preservice teacher's existing cognitive structure to accommodate experiences with perplexities. As we earlier surmised, the receptivity of one's cognitive structure to new experiences plays a key role in influencing what is learned.

Other researchers have found similar contradictions between teachers' professed beliefs and their actions in the classroom (Cohen, 1990; Cooney, 1985; Cooney, Shealy, & Arvold, 1998; Franke, Fennema, & Carpenter, 1997). Therefore, in our work with student teachers, we talk about beliefs only after they have taught their lessons. By trying to justify their instructional practice, they can get a better insight into their own beliefs.

TEACHER COGNITIVE PROCESSES

We selected three classes of thinking processes that impact instructional practice in important ways: planning, monitoring and regulating, and evaluating and revising. These processes are involved in teacher decision making and judgments before, during, and after classroom instruction. A brief description of each of these thinking processes follows with a commentary on their potential impact on classroom instruction.

Preactive Stage: Planning

Planning is the thinking that teachers do as they prepare to teach lessons. A lesson plan is a concrete embodiment of the teacher's thinking regarding the instructional activities to be enacted in the classroom. Research has demonstrated that teachers' plans are reflected in the tasks, learning environment, and indirectly, the discourse that takes place during their instructional practice (Hill, Yinger, & Robbins, 1981; Peterson, Marx, & Clark, 1978). Thus, the planning teachers engage in before instruction has the potential to impact the nature and quality of their lessons. In our exploratory study, teachers whose lesson objective was building students' conceptual and procedural understanding tended to design tasks at an appropriate level of difficulty and sequenced so as to facilitate the students' ability to extend their own learning. They tended to design lessons that incorporated the types of instructional strategies that maximize the chances for student involvement and learning with understanding. They also allotted enough time for these activities so that a comfortable environment was set within which rich interactive discourse among students occurred.

Interactive Stage: Monitoring and Regulating

Monitoring and regulating are the metacognitive strategies used to check and modify one's actions during problem solving. Research studies show that these decision-making processes play a pivotal role not only in the efficacy of the problem-solving process but also in the ultimate solution of the problem (Artzt & Armour-Thomas, 1992, 2001; Garofalo & Lester, 1985; Schoenfeld, 1987). Just as monitoring and regulating influence problem solving in critical ways, they also affect instructional practice.

Teachers who observe, listen to, and elicit the participation of students on an ongoing basis to assess student learning and disposition toward mathematics are more likely to meet the needs of their students. They do this by adapting or changing their plans based on the information they receive. For example, in our exploratory study, teachers who noticed that some students were confused during instruction often suggested the use of more concrete modes of representation to improve clarity. For example, a teacher who noticed that students were getting too talkative during a cooperative learning session realized that the task needed more structure and decided to bring the group together for spontaneous group presentations. Another teacher, while monitoring students' comments to one another during a classroom discourse and noting that the conversation was digressing too far from the objectives of the lesson, decided to change the course of the discussion by steering the students back to the initial question.

Postactive Stage: Evaluating and Revising

Evaluating and revising are two decision-making processes teachers use after their instructional practice. Teachers reexamine recently enacted lessons to determine whether the goals of instruction were achieved or not. This process enables teachers to become aware of the strengths and weaknesses of their teaching and revise classroom practices. We agree with Leiva (1995) that, "Teacher self-evaluation and the analysis of teaching are central to improving mathematics teaching within the framework of the Standards document" (p.44). Examples of how teachers' postlesson thoughts can affect their subsequent instructional practice follow.

Teachers who evaluate their lessons in terms of students' understanding of concepts and procedures and dispositions toward mathematics, as well as the effects of their instruction on these outcomes, are likely to revise their lessons in ways that will enhance student learning. For example, in our exploratory study, one teacher conducted a lesson in which she felt the contextual setting for a problem would motivate the students. After evaluating the low level of student involvement in the lesson, she suggested the use of a different setting that might be of greater interest to the students. Another teacher allotted too little time for an activity and noticed that students were not asking enough questions or debating enough issues. After evaluating the student behavior in light of the pacing, she decided to change the structure of the lesson so as to allot more time for that particular activity. After evaluating the nature of the students' questions and the students' in-class work, and believing that they revealed a lack of conceptual understanding, another teacher decided to probe deeper into the reasons for this lack of understanding. She decided to use a writing assignment in which students would explain what they did and did not understand.

To indicate how teacher knowledge, beliefs, goals, and thinking processes influence what teachers do in classrooms, the next chapter describes an exploratory research study that was done using the TCF presented thus far. This study revealed empirical evidence for some specific ways that the components of teacher cognitions influence teachers' instructional practice.

Chapter 4

Putting It All Together

This is, for the most part, a practical book. Starting in the next chapter, we'll show you how to observe lessons (including your own), reflect on them, and improve them. But you have a right to ask whether this is a valid model for examining teaching, and we have an obligation to show that it is. This chapter provides the evidence. It describes research results in which we documented the specific relationships of teachers' cognitions and their instructional practices. We also present evidence of the usefulness of the model.

In an effort to better understand the relationship between teachers' thoughts and actions in the classroom, we combined the Phase-Dimension Framework (PDF) and the Teacher Cognitions Framework (TCF) into an integrative model of teaching. The model is based on the assumption that what teachers do in the classroom is influenced by the goals they set for students, what they believe and know about teaching and learning mathematics, and the decisions they make about these matters before, during, and after classroom practice. Figure 1 illustrates the components of the model and the suggested interrelationships among them.

In an exploratory study of teachers of secondary school mathematics, we demonstrated how the model allowed us to determine some specific relationships between cognitions and instructional practices of teachers with varying levels of experience (Artzt & Armour-Thomas, 1998; Artzt,

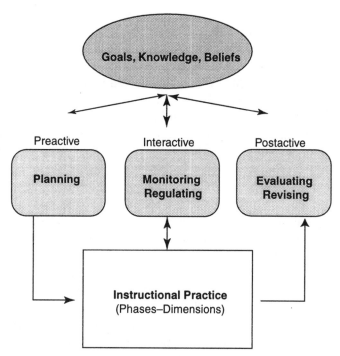

FIG. 1 Components of the model for teaching. Adapted from "A Structure to Enable Pre-service Teachers of Mathematics to Reflect on Their Teaching," by A. F. Artzt, 1999, *Journal of Mathematics Teacher Education, 2*(2), p. 145. Copyright © 1999 by Kluwer Academic Publishers. Also adapted from "Mathematics Teaching as Problem Solving," by A. F. Artzt and E. Armour-Thomas, 1998, *Instructional Science, 26*(1–2), p. 8. Copyright © 1998 by Kluwer Academic Publishers. Adapted with kind permission from Kluwer Academic Publishers.

1999). Seven experienced and seven first-year teachers of secondary school mathematics voluntarily participated in the study. The experienced teachers had taught from 7 to 25 years. The beginning teachers were student teachers from local middle schools and high schools. Teachers were asked to choose any lesson that would allow for an examination of both their classroom practice and their thoughts underlying that practice.

One author and a research assistant observed, wrote notes as they observed the lessons, and videotaped each of the teachers teaching a mathematics lesson of their own design. The observation notes provided information about classroom occurrences that might not have been visible on the videotape. Transcriptions were made of the audio part of the videotapes for analysis.

The Phase-Dimension Framework (PDF) was used to observe the lessons of these teachers. A descriptive analysis of the data allowed us to distinguish three groups of lessons. That is, specific patterns of instruction seemed to emerge and fall into two distinct groups, with a third group consisting of lessons that resembled a combination of the two other groups. For ease of discussion, these groups are labeled SC (student-centered), TC (teacher-centered), and M (mixed).

We used the Teacher Cognitions Framework (TCF) to examine the cognitions of teachers whose lessons we observed using the PDF. Following the enactment of a lesson, each teacher was asked questions about their cognitive processes: preactive cognitions (lesson planning), interactive cognitions (monitoring and regulating), and postactive cognitions (evaluating and suggesting) (Artzt & Armour-Thomas, 1998). We used these data to describe the patterns of cognitions associated with each of the three categories of lessons (student-centered, teacher-centered, mixed) that were derived from the PDF analysis.

The results are presented according to lesson groups. That is, for each group, a description of the most interesting characteristics of the lessons and the related cognitions underlying these lessons are given. (See Appendix A for summary statements of all characteristics of the lessons and related cognitions.) Woven through these descriptions are an example of one lesson from the group and the related cognitions of the teacher of that lesson. To clearly exemplify the ideas, we chose to highlight the most extreme cases.

INSTRUCTIONAL PRACTICES
AND UNDERLYING COGNITIONS OF TEACHERS
IN THE STUDENT-CENTERED (SC) GROUP

The SC group conducted five lessons: four were taught by experienced teachers, and one was taught by a first-year teacher. The descriptive analysis revealed that, the instructional practices in these lessons consistently promoted student learning with understanding across all dimensions and phases of the lessons. The teachers' expressed cognitions revealed a similar focus. That is, their articulated knowledge, beliefs, and goals centered on student learning with understanding, as did their thought processes before, during, and after the lesson.

A more detailed description of the results follows, with specific examples and quotes taken from Gina's lesson and cognitions. Gina was in her 10th year of teaching high school mathematics and was observed teaching a geometry lesson on proving overlapping triangles congruent to a class of 33 tenth graders in an urban high school.

Preactive

In their preactive interviews, teachers in the SC group revealed goals for their students to attain both procedural and conceptual understanding of the content: Gina said, "I wanted to focus in on a plan that we needed to have. Lots of times in the past, they don't know what they're doing. They don't know how to think about it, where they're going. So they have to have a definite plan." The students demonstrated knowledge of the content, pedagogical techniques, and students. Gina knew that students had difficulty visualizing overlapping triangles and was prepared to use colored chalk as an aid. She also prepared problems that, instead of requiring proofs, required only the recognition of the overlapping sections.

Interactive

The instructional practices of the teachers in the SC group were consistent with their preactive cognitions. For example, the tasks appeared to be interesting to students, logically sequenced, and at a suitable level of difficulty. Gina started with triangles that were not overlapping, went to triangles with one full overlapping part, and then moved to the more difficult case where the triangles had segments of parts overlapping. Also, most of the students in the SC group appeared to be actively involved in the tasks. Gina had the students work in pairs on several of the problems.

During their stimulated-recall interviews, these teachers made specific comments regarding their beliefs about the necessity of a student-centered approach for student learning. Gina said, "I would like them to talk more, listen to each other, because that's how you learn." Furthermore, teachers in the SC group gave descriptions of how they used student participation and feedback as a means of monitoring student understanding, which they used for subsequent regulation of instruction. The discourse during the instructional practice was consistent with these cognitions. That is, the teachers encouraged all the students to think and reason, give full explanations of their thoughts, and listen to and respond to one another's ideas. Gina said, "There are a few good students who always have their hands up. They would, if I let them, dominate the class, and nobody else would ever have time to think."

Postactive

In their debriefing interviews, the teachers in the SC group showed a consistency with their preactive goals, in that they rated their lessons primarily in terms of their evaluation of how much their students understood. Gina said, "I would have liked to have finished more. But I felt pretty good about how it went. There were a lot of hands raised. I thought they understood." Finally, the teachers gave detailed suggestions for improving their instructional techniques aimed at increasing clarity and interest for students. Gina said, "Next time, I would try using transparencies maybe. Move it around a little bit. Maybe have some cut-outs and take two overlapping triangles and put them different ways."

INSTRUCTIONAL PRACTICES
AND UNDERLYING COGNITIONS OF TEACHERS
IN THE TEACHER-CENTERED (TC) GROUP

The TC group conducted four lessons, all taught by first-year teachers. In contrast to the lessons for the SC group, the instructional practices in these lessons consistently seemed less likely to promote student learning with understanding across all dimensions and all phases of the lessons. Similarly, the expressed cognitions of these teachers were consistently focused on their own practices rather than on student learning with understanding. That is, their articulated knowledge, beliefs, and goals centered around content coverage for skill development and management concerns, as were their thought processes before, during, and after the lesson.

A more detailed description of the results follows, with specific examples taken from the lesson and cognitions of Ellen, a student teacher in an urban middle school. She was observed teaching a first lesson on graphing linear equations to a class of 26 seventh graders.

Preactive

In their preactive interviews, the teachers in the TC group expressed only procedural goals for their students and desires to cover the content. They revealed a general and vague knowledge of their students, the mathematical content, and related pedagogy. Ellen said, "The students are of average ability. Some of them have had this before, so I don't want them to get bored." The teachers spoke about the content in isolation and focused mainly on time-saving management strategies to cover the content. Ellen said, "I want my students to learn how to plot a line. I just wanted to do one example and to just get right into the graphing."

Interactive

The instructional practices of the TC group involved tasks that were illogically sequenced and either too easy or too difficult for the students. For homework, Ellen gave the students the tedious and simple task of plotting 14 pairs of points on a coordinate grid. During the lesson, she made a large leap to the idea of solving equations in two variables and gave a misleading example. Both the organization of the content and the tools used by these teachers masked the clarity of the concepts. The instructional routines, combined with pacing that was either too fast or too slow, contributed to a tense and awkward classroom atmosphere in which many of the students appeared to be off task. In Ellen's class, one by one, in a time-consuming manner, 14 different students were requested to plot their points on a small, hard-to-read coordinate grid that was placed on an overhead projector. The students at their seats were inattentive and noisy.

The verbal interactions during the TC group's lessons reflected these teachers' cognitions. The absence of monitoring for student understanding during the lessons was evidenced in the nature of the discourse. The teachers asked low-level, leading questions with wait times that were mostly too short but sometimes too long. They did not require students to give explanations of their responses, nor did they encourage interactions between students. They passed judgment on student responses and often resolved questions without student input. Throughout the lesson, Ellen asked all low-level questions, accepted responses from students who called out, and told them whether their answers were right or wrong. When a response was incorrect, she made such derogatory comments as "How could you forget that?" and then engaged in a one-on-one conversation with the student, further losing the class' attention.

During the stimulated-recall interviews, the TC group made no statements regarding their beliefs about how students learn best, unlike the SC group. They gave descriptions of how they monitored student behaviors as a means for improving classroom management but made no mention of monitoring for student understanding. In fact, none of these teachers described or made any deviations from the original plans, despite feedback from students during the course of the lesson that indicated they were confused. Ellen seemed bewildered by the students' incorrect responses and explained it by saying, "I think he wasn't thinking," and "They don't think."

Postactive

In their debriefing interviews, the teachers in the TC group showed a consistency with their preactive goals in that their primary focus was on their insufficient content coverage and the behavior of the students. Ellen said, "I didn't get to cover as much as I thought. I thought it would go quicker. There wasn't enough time to summarize, to put it all together at the end. I think the kids were very good today. But some kids were still not paying as much attention as I'd like." Several gave suggestions for improvement of the pacing of their lessons to achieve more efficient content coverage. Ellen said, "Next time I would not require the students to organize the data pairs in a table since it took so long."

INSTRUCTIONAL PRACTICES AND UNDERLYING COGNITIONS OF TEACHERS OF THE MIXED (M) GROUP

The M group conducted five lessons: three were taught by experienced teachers, and two were taught by first-year teachers. These lessons were assigned to the M group because each lesson had components that resembled those of both the SC and TC groups. In each lesson, the nature of the instructional practice was fairly inconsistent. A descriptive analysis revealed a similar inconsistency in the focus of the expressed cognitions of these teachers. In some essential characteristics, to be explained subsequently, the lessons and cognitions of three of the teachers, two experienced and one beginning (to be referred to as the M1 group), were similar, and the lessons and cognitions of two of the teachers, one experienced and one beginning (to be referred to as the M2 group), were similar.

M1 Group

The tasks and learning environments of the lessons for the M1 group were similar to those of the lessons in the SC group, but the discourse was more similar to the lessons in the TC group. More specifically, a teacher-dominated style of discourse prevailed in which little monitoring for student understanding occurred during any phase of the lesson. Similarity among the beliefs of these teachers shed light on their instructional practices.

A more detailed description of the results follows, with specific examples taken from Betty's lesson and cognitions. Betty was in her 17th year of teaching secondary school mathematics. She was observed teaching a geometry lesson on proving the properties of isosceles triangles to a class of 22 tenth graders in a suburban high school.

Preactive

In their preactive interviews, the three teachers from the M1 group revealed goals for their students similar to those of the SC group. That is, they wanted students to develop conceptual as well as procedural understanding of the content. Betty said, "I wanted to reinforce previous concepts and to get the students to realize what does happen in an isosceles triangle." Teachers in the M1 group exhibited detailed knowledge about their pupils, the content, and related pedagogy. Betty stated, "I know the speed at which to go with this class." She said that, in fact, she was not in a rush since "we're right on target with time."

Interactive

With respect to the tasks and most aspects of the learning environments, the instructional practices of each of the three teachers from the M1 group resembled the instructional practices of the SC group. That is, throughout all lesson phases, the tasks were logically sequenced and at a suitable level of difficulty. The tools used and the organization of tasks contributed to the clarity of the lessons. Betty had handouts prepared for the students that contained accurately drawn triangles with problems of increasing difficulty. Teachers in the M1 group handled administrative routines effectively without disrupting their students who were doing their assigned work. While students completed the handout, Betty checked attendance, walked around checking homework, and also checked their progress on the handout to select students to put their work on the board.

With respect to discourse, however, the instructional practices of the M1 group resembled that of the TC group. That is, discourse was normally fast paced and not conducive to student input. Betty's overriding questioning technique was to ask a student a question, allow a very short wait time, accept a one-word answer from the student, and then give the explanation for the student's answer herself.

During their stimulated-recall interviews, the teachers in the M1 group revealed beliefs quite different from those expressed by the teachers in the SC group, who valued the student-centered approach to teaching. Both of the experienced M1 group teachers stated that to cover the content efficiently, a more teacher-centered approach was desirable. That is, they believed it was best to tell students the information rather than spend the time getting them to discover it for themselves. Betty stated, "Sometimes I let students explain their work. But because of time factors, I took charge. It works well when the teacher stands in front of the room and answers student questions." Note that this view seemed inconsistent with her preactive assertion that time was not a problem. The first-year teacher expressed her uncertainty regarding how much to elicit from students and how much to tell them, in light of the time constraints of a class period and her concerns about covering the content. Similar to the TC group, all three M1 group teachers explained that the primary reason they called on students was to keep them on task.

Postactive

In their debriefing interviews, the teachers in the M1 group evaluated their lessons as the TC group had, in terms of content coverage ("I accomplished what I wanted to") and gave suggestions for improvement that focused on ways to accomplish more efficient pacing. This was inconsistent with their preactive cognitions that, similar to those in the SC group, focused on helping students to attain procedural as well as conceptual understanding.

M2 Group

During the initiation phases of the two lessons conducted by the M2 group, the tasks, learning environments, and discourse were all similar to the SC group's lessons. However, during the development and closure phases, the discourse was similar to the TC group's lessons. Similarity in the extent of the knowledge they revealed shed light on this instructional practice.

A more detailed description of the results follows, with specific examples taken from the lesson and cognitions of John, a student teacher in an urban middle school. He was observed teaching a lesson on plotting points on a rectangular coordinate system to a class of 30 seventh grade students.

Preactive

Similar to the SC group, in their preactive interviews, the two teachers in the M2 group revealed goals for their students to develop conceptual as well as procedural understanding of the content. John said, "My main objective is to get the students to plot the points, to connect them, and review geometric concepts and understand the relations." The M2 group also expressed beliefs about the importance of having students play an active role in their own learning by asking them questions and challenging them to think for themselves and interact with one another. John said, "If a kid can do it, I prefer if he explains. It helps him." However, unlike the teachers in the SC group, the teachers in the M2 group either admitted to or demonstrated that they had inadequate or superficial knowledge about some aspects of the content, students, and/or pedagogy. John revealed only a general and vague knowledge of his students by anticipating that "it would be an easy lesson and [he] wouldn't have any difficulty." To accomplish his goals, John said, "I plan to help them to do it instead of to do it myself. I'm going to send them to the board."

Interactive

During the initiation phase of the lessons given by the M2 group, the tasks, learning environments, and discourse resembled those of the SC group's lessons. However, during the development and closure phases of their lessons, the tasks and discourse resembled those of the TC group's lessons. That is, the tasks were either too difficult or confusing for students, the discourse was teacher centered, and the instructional routines and pacing were teacher dominated and not conducive to student input. After students explained their work on plotting pairs of points to one another at the board, John assigned a complex problem that required students to plot four given points, join them, and find the perimeter and area of the resulting figure. The students showed a lack of familiarity with the concepts of perimeter and area. Therefore, John was unable to elicit the responses he wanted in the short time remaining. He resorted to telling the students how to do the problem and gave them the answers as the bell rang. Because the students did not have the prerequisite understanding of the concepts of perimeter and area, the quick "telling" did not seem to help them understand.

As they watched the videotape of the initiation phase of their lessons, the teachers in the M2 group, similar to the SC group, claimed that they called on students to check for understanding and determine how to proceed. John said, "I was trying to see if they were able to do the Do Now, because if they couldn't do it, forget it. And I saw that some of them had some difficulty." However, as they watched the development and closure phases of their lessons, the teachers in the M2 group remarked that the tasks they introduced caused confusion, which required them to tell the students the information. John said, "I was thinking how long this part is going to take me since the students didn't understand, but I have to do it since it's on the homework so I just had to tell them."

Postactive

In their debriefing interviews, both teachers in the M2 group, similar to the SC group, evaluated student understanding and gave appropriate suggestions for how to improve the design of the tasks in their lessons. John admitted, "I was too ambitious. I'm not sure that many knew what was going on. I should have just focused on plotting points and not include area and perimeter." Both teachers claimed that their inadequate knowledge of the content, students, and/or pedagogy impeded their efforts to teach in a way that was consistent with their goals and beliefs.

Through the application of our model, we were able to discern differences in instructional practices and use teacher cognitions as a way of better understanding the nature of these differences. That is, patterns of cognitions paralleled differences in the nature of instructional practices.

CONCLUSION

The purpose of this exploratory study was to use a "teaching for understanding" perspective to develop a model to examine teachers' instructional practices in secondary school mathematics in relationship to their underlying cognitions. We used the Phase-Dimension Framework to differentiate 14 mathematics lessons. We then engaged in a systematic examination of the cognitions of the teachers of these lessons.

Using the Phase-Dimension Framework, lessons were partitioned into three categories based on the dimensions of teaching (tasks, learning environment, discourse) across the three phases of instruction (initiation, development, closure). By examining teachers' cognitions, some insights were gained regarding the variations in the nature of the instructional practice of these lessons. In many ways, the results presented here are in alignment with the results found by researchers who have studied changes in mathematics teachers' beliefs and practices (e.g., Cooney, Shealy, & Arvold, 1998; Fennema, Carpenter, Frank, Levi, Jacobs, & Empson, 1996; Schifter & Simon, 1992; Schram, Wilcox, Lappan, & Lanier, 1989;

Thompson, 1991). These researchers all agree that there appear to be several developmental stages of teaching. These stages are somewhat evident in the cognitions and instructional practices of the teachers of lessons grouped in this study.

The instructional practices and cognitions of the teachers in the SC group in many ways exemplified those of teachers who have developed beyond the initial stage of teaching. In these classes, there were rich verbal exchanges among the students and between the students and the teachers. The teachers engaged in extensive monitoring of the verbal interactions and behaviors of students throughout their class sessions. This close monitoring may have accounted for their subsequent accurate postlesson judgments regarding whether they had accomplished their goals of teaching for student understanding. These teachers' monitoring behaviors were similar to those of expert teachers (Leinhardt & Greeno, 1986; Livingston & Borko, 1990) and good problem solvers (Schoenfeld, 1987; Silver, 1985). It was encouraging to note that these competencies, usually associated with expertise, were exhibited by one of the beginning teachers. This has positive implications for preservice teachers. That is, although experience plays an important role in the development of a teacher, it is possible for a beginning teacher to think and teach in ways that place students at the center of instruction.

In contrast, the instructional practices and cognitions of the teachers in the TC group at best resembled that of initial stage teachers. Initial stage teaching has been characterized as traditional instruction by teachers driven by the belief that students learn best by receiving clear information transmitted by a knowledgeable teacher (Goldsmith & Shifter, 1997). For example, there were relatively no verbal interactions between students, and those that occurred between the teacher and students were minimal. Providing little room for the expression of student ideas prevented these teachers from being able to monitor the level or quality of their students' understanding of the mathematical ideas. This lack of monitoring may have accounted for the inaccurate postlesson judgments these teachers made that their lesson went well or that their students understood. In many ways, the four first-year teachers in the TC group exhibited behaviors similar to those of other novice teachers (Borko & Livingston, 1989; Livingston & Borko, 1990) and naive problem solvers (Hinsley, Hayes, & Simon, 1977). For preservice teachers, these findings indicate that if the goal of instruction is student understanding, then one way to assess whether this goal has been accomplished is by consistently monitoring student understanding throughout the lesson.

The teachers in the M group revealed a lack of consistency within or among components of their cognitions. For some lessons, the teachers expressed knowledge and goals consistent with teaching to promote student understanding. However, their lack of monitoring for student understanding during the interactive stage of teaching was inconsistent with these preactive cognitions. Furthermore, they showed an unawareness of the lack of coherence between their postlesson cognitions, which focused only on content coverage and more efficient pacing in subsequent lessons, and their preactive cognitions, which focused on student understanding. Teachers' beliefs about the value of "teacher telling" may have accounted for the persistent use of teacher-dominated strategies for discourse, which resulted in the absence of monitoring for student understanding across all phases of their lessons. During their debriefing interviews, they expressed the belief that when they have limited time, covering the content efficiently must take precedence over student learning with understanding. Similar to the teachers in Lampert's work (1985), these teachers were unable to maintain the "tension" between simultaneously covering the content and attending to student understanding. Coping effectively with this apparent paradox of teaching remains an important challenge for teachers.

Other teachers in the M group revealed beliefs and goals that suggested the importance of student learning with understanding. However, because of their inadequate or superficial knowledge about the content, students, and/or pedagogy, in the development and closure phases of their lessons, they were unable to monitor and regulate their classroom teaching in a manner consistent with their preactive cognitions. For teachers of these lessons, regardless of experience, their major source of difficulties seem to have been weaknesses in different aspects of their knowledge. Research suggests that teacher knowledge plays a prominent role in the nature of instructional practice (cf., Peterson, 1988; Shulman, 1986). Specifically, after the initial phase of their lessons, when they realized that they had introduced tasks that were causing confusion for themselves or for their students and did not know how to adjust the tasks, the M group resorted to teacher-centered lessons. One might say that a teacher-directed style of teaching can serve as a mask for teachers who do not possess full knowledge of the content, students, and/or pedagogy. That is, without the demands that arise from student input, teachers are free to impose the material on the students even when they themselves do not fully understand it or have inappropriately sequenced the material. With the present emphasis on the critical role of discourse for the teaching of mathematics with understanding, it is ever more important that you develop a thorough and integrated knowledge system.

The absence of monitoring for student understanding was a common weakness in the lessons conducted by the TC group, and in all or parts of the lessons in the M group. A greater weakness may be these teachers' apparent unawareness of the importance of monitoring for student understanding as a way to accurately make postlesson judgments of student understanding. This has important implications for beginning teachers because accurate postlesson assessments of student understanding are an important means of obtaining more information about students for subsequent planning and classroom practice. Monitoring student understanding and appropriately regulating instruction are key factors in the nature of teachers' instructional practice and their potential for professional growth. Researchers on problem solving support this notion of the critical role of cognitive monitoring and subsequent regulation in the efficacy of the problem-solving process and in the ultimate solution of the problem (Artzt & Armour-Thomas, 1992; Garofalo & Lester, 1985; Schoenfeld, 1987).

Although we are excited by the promising nature of our work, it is only an exploratory study, and we are aware of its limitations. Nevertheless, through the use of the model, we were able to examine the teaching of mathematics as an integrated whole and obtain a better understanding of instructional practices and associated teacher cognitions. We have used the model in our teacher education program as a vehicle through which our student teachers systematically reflect on their mathematics teaching as well as their underlying cognitions (Artzt, 1999). According to the research on teacher change, such systematic reflection and self-assessment can be a powerful facilitator of teacher improvement (Jaworski, 1994; Kemmis, 1985; Schon, 1983).

This model linking teachers' cognitions with their instructional practices serves as the conceptual basis for the reflective and self-assessment activities you will engage in during your year of teacher preparation. The model will be the foundation for your observations of other teachers, for observations you and others do of your own teaching, and for the portfolio you will create. Part II of this book describes the structure for each of these activities in detail and in some cases provides samples of the work of our student teachers.

Part II

HOW TO USE THE MODEL

Chapter **5**

Using the Model to Examine
the Instructional Practice
and Cognitions of Other
Teachers

One of the most valuable experiences that should precede teaching and continue throughout a teaching career is observing other teachers. Observations can sensitize you to some of the critical aspects of instructional practice and their relationship to teachers' cognitions. Because teaching is such a complex endeavor, observations must be done with a specific focus grounded in a theoretical framework. This chapter describes 10 structured observations of lessons taught in local secondary schools. Each of the first 9 observations focuses on a critical aspect of instructional practice in mathematics: the nature of the mathematical content, questioning, motivation and teaching strategies, homework, use of class time, verbal behavior of students, task orientation of students, assessment, and teacher expectations and stereotyping. (Notice that we have arranged these observations so that they first focus primarily on the content, then on the teacher, and then on the individual students. However, because all aspects of instruction are deeply interrelated, these observations can certainly be sequenced differently.) Each of these aspects of instruction is identified by elements within the model. For example, for the observation on questioning, the specific dimension of instructional practice to be examined is discourse. Although each of these aspects of instructional practice concern all the dimensions of teaching (tasks, learning environment, and discourse), the preactive (planning) and interactive (monitoring and regulating) stages of teaching, and the phases of teaching (initiation, development, closure), some are more directly related to one dimension, phase, or stage than another. Therefore, although the observation might focus on discourse, other areas such as monitoring, regulating, and possibly the learning environment come into play as well. Each observation also considers the probable teacher cognitions that accompanied the observed practice. The 10th observation uses the entire model and encompasses all the dimensions, phases, and stages of the lesson and conjectures for the teacher's cognitions that drive the lesson.

Each observation assignment includes a rationale for the assignment, a summary of the observation procedure, and an example of a student teacher's work on the observation. Appendix B presents detailed forms for all the observations presented in this chapter. It is important that before doing each observation, you do the readings in your methods text regarding the topic of the observation. That way you will bring a more informed understanding to your interpretation of what you are viewing. For example, if you are doing an observation that asks you to evaluate discourse, you should read the section in your text that discusses questioning.

OBSERVATION 1:
NATURE OF THE CONTENT (TASKS)

Mathematics is an exciting and dynamic area of study that offers students the chance to use the power of their minds. It is essential that teachers engage students in tasks that exemplify the beauty and usefulness of mathematics. What teachers know and believe about mathematics strongly influence what they do in the classroom and ultimately what students learn about mathematics. In addition, teachers' knowledge and beliefs about mathematics shape their goals for student learning.

Observation Procedure

This first observation is designed to sensitize you to the messages students are receiving about what mathematics is and what is of importance to learn. You are encouraged to use the mathematical tasks you observe as a basis for making conjectures about the cognitions of the teacher. Observation 1 includes the following steps:

1. Observe the mathematical content of the lesson from two perspectives:

      a. Examine the accuracy of the content and make any corrections with respect to the mathematical errors, misconceptions, or misrepresentations you observe.

      b. Examine the extent to which the teacher explicitly points out the value of the mathematical content that the students are learning. That is, does the teacher indicate the importance of mathematics as the study of patterns, the language of science, a system of abstract ideas or how mathematics helps us to understand the world around us?

2. Based on these observations, make conjectures regarding the teacher's knowledge of mathematics, his or her beliefs about the nature of mathematics, and his or her goals for what the students should learn about mathematics.

Observation Example

Elise observed a lesson in logic and although there were no mathematical errors, she found the lesson lacking because it did not point out the value of learning the logical rules. The lesson required students to determine whether certain arguments were valid by transliterating them into symbols and then comparing them to the Laws of Modus Tollens and the Law of Detachment that were written symbolically on the board.

> I was almost shocked at how neglected the mentioning of any values was. I was especially surprised because I felt that a lesson in logic lends itself most easily and naturally to explicitly stating the value of the material. After all, logical thinking and decoding of statements to determine truth values and necessary consequences is something everyone does a hundred times a day. How invigorating to see that a mathematical transliteration of everyday occurrences into a precise symbolic representation can make us able to clearly analyze our everyday environment, interactions, patterns of thought, and more!

Clearly, Elise has a genuine appreciation for the value of learning logic.

Elise pointed out that the teacher made reference to the usefulness of what the students were learning but did not make it come alive when they discussed the sample problem:

> The most I can say is that the teacher once told the students that if they learn how to do this, they will be able to analyze if what a friend is

telling them is the truth or not. However, she didn't demonstrate how, or give an example, or show how the examples they were discussing was an instance of that opportunity. It was clear that the students did not understand that what they were doing would in fact make them able to do such a thing. For example, one word problem asked the students to state if the following argument was valid, and if so, which law was being illustrated. The argument was:

If you're voted MVP, you win a trophy.

Cathy won a trophy.

Therefore, Cathy was voted MVP.

Rather than discussing the situation and leading the students to intu-itively get the answer and then show how the system of transliteration and the fact that there is no such law that corresponds because the argu-ment is not valid, the teacher had them robotically transliterate the incor-rect argument, then compare it to the laws on the board, and conclude that the argument isn't valid because the symbols don't match. It was clear to me that the majority of the students had no connection between the actual argument and the symbols on the board!

Elise was sensitive to the strict, abstract procedural approach the teacher took and had good ideas for improving on this approach in a way that would help students appreciate the value of the mathematical con-cepts they were learning:

Throughout the period I was thinking of ways to make the students understand and appreciate what they were learning to do. For example, before having them transliterate into symbols, I'd have tried to lead them to the conclusion that the argument was invalid. For example, I'd ask them things like: Is it true that just because Cathy won a trophy, it means she must have been voted MVP? Is it possible that she got a tro-phy but wasn't voted MVP? Can you think of such a situation? OK, now let's see how our systematic representation and mathematical logi-cal argumentation leads us straight to what your intuition is telling you. At that point we would transliterate it, and seeing that it wasn't one of the laws, we would see that you can't conclude for sure that Cathy was voted MVP.

At this point I would show them how this was an example of how mathematics helps us to understand our environment. You see, if Cathy had come up to you and said, "If you're voted MVP, you win a trophy. See, here's my trophy—I was voted MVP!" You'll know she's not necessarily telling you the truth! She could've gotten the trophy for something else! On the other hand, you'll know she's not necessarily lying either. This is a perfect opportunity to express to the students how amazing it is that this system of mathematical logic aids us in our societal interactions.

Elise's suggestions show that she has a deep understanding of and appreciation for the laws of logic. Regarding the teacher's level of appreciation, Elise said, "Judging from this lesson, I feel that this teacher thinks about mathematics as an arbitrary set of rules disconnected from experience. His goals seem to be to make sure that his students know how to apply this set of rules." Elise's comment not only reveals her awareness of how devoid of meaning this lesson was, but also she gives specific ways to make it more meaningful to students. Of course, one lesson cannot reveal a teacher's entire knowledge of or beliefs about mathematics. However, Elise has begun to think about this teacher's cognitions and how they may have contributed to the nature of this particular lesson. The next observation assignment concerns the discourse that occurs within the mathematics class.

OBSERVATION 2: QUESTIONING (DISCOURSE)

Discourse is a critical aspect of the mathematics classroom and is central to the current vision of desirable mathematics teaching (NCTM 1989, 1991, 2000). The teacher's role today is to create a mathematical "discourse community" (Silver & Smith, 1996). Specifically, according to the Professional Teaching Standards (NCTM, 1991), the teacher should

- Pose questions that elicit, engage, and challenge each student's thinking.
- Listen carefully to students' ideas and ask them to clarify and justify their ideas.
- Encourage students to listen to, respond to, and question the teacher and one another.

Student teachers generally find discourse to be the most critical ingredient for satisfying teaching experiences but the most difficult part of their work. Discourse happens in unique ways in each class and involves instantaneous decision making. A good start in learning how to orchestrate discourse is examining the discourse that takes place in other teachers' classes.

Observation Procedure

This observation is divided into two parts. The first part requires that you observe the questioning style of the teacher.

1. Describe the nature of each question the teacher asks. Is the question convergent or divergent? What is the form of the question? Is it a yes/no question? Is it a leading question? (See Posamentier & Stepelman, 1999, pp. 75–84 for descriptions of different question types.)
2. Describe the percentage of all responses that are chorus responses, individually volunteered responses, or individually teacher-selected responses.
3. Keep track of the wait time for each question. Research (Rowe, 1974) suggests that wait time affects the quantity and quality of responses given by students, so it is an important variable to consider when examining a teacher's method of questioning.
4. Decide how the method of questioning affected the verbal communication that took place in the classroom.
5. Consider how it affected the learning that took place among the different students.
6. Suggest how the questioning might be improved to better meet the learning needs of each of the students.
7. Make conjectures regarding the teacher cognitions that might have contributed to the questions the teacher asked. What could have contributed to the teacher's level of questions? That is, did the teacher only ask low-level questions because of inadequate knowledge of the content or because of beliefs about the students and their inability to learn?

The second part of this observation focuses more closely on the discourse structure of the lesson. Much research has been done in this area, as reported by Cazden (1986).

1. Attend to the specific roles of the teacher and the students in initiating the questions, providing the responses, and reconceptualizing the ideas put forth during the classroom discourse. Keep a tally of

a. Each time the teacher or a student requests an answer or an explanation.

b. Each time the teacher or a student states an answer or an explanation.

c. Each time the teacher or a student rephrases a question or an explanation, expands on a question or an explanation, restates a question or an explanation, or evaluates someone else's question or explanation.

2. Using the data you have gathered, make a bar graph that compares the teacher's and the students' conversational contributions.

a. Analyze the nature of the classroom discourse.

b. Discuss what it might reveal about the teacher's beliefs regarding the teacher's and the students' roles in the classroom discourse.

c. Suggest ways to change the discourse so that it will contribute to increased student learning.

Observation Example

Olive observed two eleventh grade honors classes, each taught by a different teacher. Regarding the first class she observed, she made the following comments in the first section of her observation:

> While observing the classroom, I noticed that the teacher primarily asked questions that required a chorus response. The teacher asked over 30 questions, and only 3 were addressed to specific students. The teacher generally had his back toward the students when asking questions. This caused him to primarily ask chorus response questions since he could not see if a student was volunteering to answer a question.

Olive saw the connection between the teacher's position in the classroom and the nature of his questioning. She also detected the factual nature of the questions and the form in which they were asked:

> The teacher's questions were over 80 percent factual and convergent and consisted mainly of whiplash and leading questions. These are examples of the type of questions that occurred frequently: And the what? Which would be what? And all this really does is what? Wouldn't you say they are equal? He usually expected a chorus response to these questions and gave students about half a second to respond to the question. I did not hear any questions that required the students to think beyond recalling past information learned.

Olive expressed her thoughts about the beliefs that she felt contributed to the teacher's "poor" questioning style:

> I suppose, due to the fact that it is an honors math course, the speed in
> which the material has to be covered must be fast. The teacher probably
> believes that the best way to cover all the material and at the same time
> involve the kids a little bit is to use the chorus-response type of question.
> By keeping the questions straightforward, he can get most of the kids to
> respond quickly and then just move along. He probably thinks that since
> they are smart kids, they can learn it this way.

Olive had some insightful comments regarding both suggestions for
ways to improve the questioning and her beliefs about how to teach honors classes:

> Before suggesting my ideas for improving the questioning, I want to say
> that I think that more than other kids, bright students need to be given a
> chance to think about hard questions. They should be challenged more
> and not just be given a fast set of procedures to follow. If they are so
> smart, they can practice more of the examples on their own time and dis-
> cuss interesting concepts during the lesson. At the very least, the teacher
> should turn away from the board and ask more interesting questions
> directed at individual students. Rather than him reviewing an assigned
> problem, he could allow the students to explain their own work.

Even if Olive's conjecture about this teacher's beliefs was faulty, the
important thing is that she recognized the connections between the
teacher's style of questioning, how it meets the needs of the individual
learners, the thoughts of the teacher, and the dilemma teachers face when
presented with a crowded curriculum.

Olive completed the second section of this observation on the second
class she observed. Again, she noticed a very teacher-centered style of discourse:

> As you can see from my graph in this lesson, the conversation was
> mostly like this: The teacher requested an answer and one of the students
> gave the answer, or a student requested an explanation and the teacher
> gave the explanation. Only twice did students give an explanation of
> anything, and only once did the teacher request an explanation. So most
> of the time, the teacher was explaining and explaining, and the students

were only either giving short answers or asking questions. I was disappointed that in such a bright class, the students were not given the chance to do some of the explaining. I'm sure many of them could have done it and would have learned something in the process. Also, never were students given the chance to answer another student's question. The teacher always took it upon himself to answer all of the students' questions.

Olive's ideas for changing the discourse conformed with a more student-centered approach. She said, "I think that after a student gave an answer, the teacher should have asked the student to explain it better. I also think that when a student asked the teacher for an explanation, sometimes the teacher should have asked the other students if any of them could explain it."

Olive had strong ideas about what this teacher's beliefs might have been:

I think this teacher believed that he alone could give the best explanation of the material and that the students would learn it better if he explained it. I think he really cared about the students and made them feel comfortable enough to ask him lots of questions. But he did not give them enough credit for being able to contribute worthwhile ideas or good explanations. I also don't think that he believed, or maybe he just never thought about, the fact that it would help the students learn if they gave an explanation. Or maybe he believed it would take longer to let the students explain anything and he was in a rush to cover the content.

Olive sees the relationship between a teacher-dominated style of discourse and the teacher's belief about his role in the classroom.

Often secondary school students share the belief that it is the teacher's role to be the "explainer." After being taught this way in the past, students believe their role is to sit quietly in the class, acting as passive receivers of information. Getting students to become active participants in their own learning involves addressing their beliefs about the role of their teachers and their role as students.

The next observation assignment concerns the motivational and teaching strategies that are used within the mathematics class. These strategies are connected with all three dimensions of classroom instruction: tasks, learning environment, and discourse.

OBSERVATION 3: MOTIVATION AND TEACHING STRATEGIES (TASKS, LEARNING ENVIRONMENT, DISCOURSE)

Motivation is a key aspect of good instructional practice. Without motivation, it is difficult, if not impossible, for student learning to occur. While motivation is a complex area of study dealing with such topics as achievement motivation, social motivation, extrinsic motivation, and intrinsic motivation, the teacher still plays a pivotal role in motivating students to learn. That is, the teacher can design lessons that maximize the chances that students' interest and curiosity will be aroused and thus be motivated to learn a particular concept. Through the use of effective teaching strategies and interesting questions, teachers can create powerful motivations for students. Of course, teachers can only accomplish this if they are convinced that it is their responsibility to do so. Teachers who believe that students should come to school motivated to learn and succeed usually believe that students are motivated by being given problems that will prepare them to do well on upcoming examinations. Unfortunately, such an attitude is only accurate for the small number of students who are high achievers. In addition, using the carrot of "doing well on an exam" as a reason for learning may prevent students from ever understanding or appreciating the real value of the material they are learning. To accept the responsibility for motivation, teachers must have a deep knowledge of the content and related effective pedagogical strategies. They must also know their students' abilities and interests to be able to design motivational questions that will be at an appropriate level of difficulty and of interest to them. A first step in learning about motivation is to observe it in others' classrooms.

Observation Procedure

In preparation for this observation, we suggest you read about motivation and effective teaching strategies in your methods text. Then, using what you have learned from your reading, you can begin the observation.

1. Describing the type of motivational techniques the teacher used and the teaching strategies he or she used to create and sustain the motivation.
2. Identify the motivational question or questions that the teacher asked. While it is true that the use of diagrams, manipulatives, calculators, and or computers may capture the attention of students, they are only tools for

learning concepts and should not be confused with motivation. Tools have maximum value when they are used to answer a specific question or set of questions. It is these questions that create the motivation to explore, discover, learn. The term problem-centered instruction used by proponents of the recent reform movement is really another way of describing a lesson that has a motivational basis. We hope that this observation will sensitize you to the critical role of motivational questions in the design of a lesson.

3. Keep your eyes pinned on the students to determine whether they seem motivated. Although a question or strategy may appear motivating to you, the students may not agree. Do the students' behaviors suggest that they are indeed motivated? How can you determine this?

4. Make suggestions for improving the motivational aspects of the lesson. For example, you might suggest changes you would make to a motivational question and suggest ways to help sustain the motivation more effectively.

5. Make conjectures regarding the teacher's beliefs about motivation and his or her knowledge of the students' abilities and interests.

Observation Example

Ellen described the class she observed as follows:

> I observed a second-semester ninth grade class consisting of students who had not passed the course or the Regents last semester. When discussing the class and motivational techniques used by the teacher, I think it is important to keep in mind the size of the class (only 19 students are registered in the class; of those, only 12 came to class, and of those 12, 3 went to the nurse) and the aforementioned achievement level of the class.

Ellen recognized the importance of knowing the students you are dealing with when considering issues of motivation. Ellen also noticed a level of motivation that was not requested in the observation report:

> The class started by having the students work on a Do Now written on the board while the teacher spot-checked the students' homework. Many of the students did not do their homework, and the teacher asked them why they had bothered coming to class at all. The students responded by asking where else could they be, and the teacher responded that they could be flipping burgers at McDonalds. Although this was not directly a

motivation for learning mathematics, it did send a message that if the students did not take advantage of attending school, they may end up in a dissatisfying position in life.

Ellen described what she considered was the main motivation of the lesson:

> The main motivation of the class was the Do Now. It consisted of two examples of factoring polynomials followed by five examples of multiplying binomials together. Three of the latter examples were the difference of two squares, which the students had never before (or rather never this semester) encountered. Students were given some time to work on the examples and were then called on (involuntarily) to write their answers on the board. After all the answers were written and verified (by the teacher and the students) the teacher asked the class why did some answers have two terms and others have three terms? She waited for an answer, but the class was quiet for a little while. I felt that this question was motivating because it presented a challenge to the students, as well as indicating a void in their knowledge.

It is clear that Ellen has a keen eye for motivation. She noticed that it was not the problems themselves that were motivating but rather the question that the teacher posed regarding the solutions to these problems. That is, the students were being asked to engage in analysis of what seemed like a surprising situation. It is also interesting that Ellen connected the students' quietness with their being motivated. Perhaps the students also had thoughtful looks on their faces that made Ellen so convinced that they were indeed interested in the question.

Ellen explained how the teacher's questioning style sustained the motivation of this class:

> A few students made some random guesses, and the teacher did not evaluate these. Instead, she asked the class to create a problem multiplying two binomials to produce a two-termed product. This question again was motivating in that it presented a challenge. One student suggested $(x + 3)(x - 5)$. The teacher wrote this on the board and asked the class to check the product. When the students informed the teacher that the product was three-termed, the teacher asked why and what happened? That question went unanswered and instead a student said that the example

had to be $(x + 3)(x - 3)$. This was verified by the students at their desks to produce a two-termed answer. This example was motivating because not only did it present a challenge, but it also got the students actively involved in justifying mathematical curiosities.

Even though Ellen believed the motivation she observed was quite effective, she still had ideas for improvement:

In general I felt that the questions asked in the Do Now were motivating for the aforementioned reasons, though they could have been even better if they had been asked in a different order. For example, the first few questions of the Do Now could have been multiplying binomials, including a few examples of differences of squares. Those questions could have then been followed by a few factoring problems, including one or two differences of squares. This would have more clearly pointed out a void in the students' knowledge.

Ellen also had suggestions for using teaching strategies that would have gotten more of the students actively involved and motivated to learn:

Another way of approaching this lesson would have been to split the class into groups, and each person in the group could have been given a couple of multiplication [of binomials] examples, including one that resulted in a difference of two squares. The group assignment might be to either write down their observations (that is, ask the question, "Why do some of these products have two terms while others have three terms?"), or try to factor a difference of two squares. Each group may then present their results. This would not only have gotten the students more actively involved in solving a problem but could also foster their motivation to learn the topic.

Ellen recognized the possibility that the teacher's knowledge of her own students and the class might have been the reason that she structured the lesson as she did and that in fact her own idea might not have worked as well:

I don't know how well my suggestions could have worked considering this class' achievement level. Perhaps this teacher knew that it was necessary to guide them more, as she did. Perhaps this teacher knew the desires of her students and how they related to each other and felt the group format would not be effective for them. She probably knew that the small class size enabled her to give every student her attention and get every student involved.

Finally, Ellen appeared sensitive in her conjectures about this teacher's beliefs about motivation:

> I was impressed with how little the teacher had to do to motivate these students. I think this teacher really understood the fact that you don't need any gimmicks or toys to motivate even these low-achieving kids. This teacher probably believes that these kids, and probably all kids, are motivated by questions that they find curious and that are within their ability to figure out. Unlike many teachers of low-ability students, this teacher still believes in their ability and desire to think.

The next observation assignment concerns the homework procedures that are a part of every mathematics class. Because homework involves a selection of tasks, a method of review, and techniques of assessment, it cannot be discussed without addressing all three dimensions of classroom instruction—tasks, learning environment, and discourse—as well as lesson phases and monitoring and regulating.

OBSERVATION 4: HOMEWORK (TASKS, LEARNING ENVIRONMENT, DISCOURSE, PHASES, MONITORING, REGULATING)

The tasks assigned to students to be completed in the privacy of their own homes play a critical role in mathematics instruction. Homework is one way of getting students actively involved in their learning of mathematics. Mathematics is not a spectator sport. Students need to practice doing many different types of problems if they are to gain proficiency and understanding of the content. Often students claim that they understand the material when it is discussed in class, but when they go home to try some problems on their own, they cannot do them. When the teacher carefully selects problems, the homework can be an effective vehicle for students to find out what they do and do not understand. If students can identify their areas of confusion to themselves, their peers, and/or their teachers, they are in a better position to be helped. It is a good time for them to practice what they have learned how to do, to find out what they do not understand, and to make discoveries on their own. The problems assigned for homework should not be limited to practice of the day's lesson alone. They might include review of past concepts; work that will set the stage for future learning; problems that will take time and last over the course of several days, weeks, or even months; or work that involves problem solving, research, and/or discovery.

Of course, creating an assignment is only the first part of the homework process. The teacher has the responsibility for allotting the time and means for students to discuss the work they have done on their own (discourse). The teacher also orchestrates what procedure is used (learning environment) and during what phase of the lesson it is done. Review of homework can range from having students discuss their work in small groups, to having different students present their work to the class as a whole, to discussing only problems that are requested by students. Each method has its unique advantages and disadvantages, and the method chosen by the teacher is usually a reflection of his or her goals for student learning, beliefs about how students learn best, and knowledge of the students.

Another part of the homework process concerns assessment (monitoring and regulating). Does the teacher check whether each of the students has done the homework? If so, what criteria are used? Does the teacher collect the homework? If so, does the teacher collect all students' homework or just a subset of the students' homework? How often is homework collected? Is it checked for accuracy or for neatness? Is it graded? Does the teacher write comments on the homework or merely place check marks at the top? As with the procedures for reviewing homework, the different procedures used for assessing homework each have their own advantages and disadvantages, and the method that the teacher chooses is usually a reflection of his or her own overarching cognitions.

A first step in learning about the aspects of assigning, reviewing, and assessing homework is to observe the different procedures that other teachers use in their mathematics classrooms.

Observation Procedure

Observation 4 includes the following steps:

1. Describe the content of the homework assignment.
2. Describe the procedure used for going over the homework.

3. Describe the procedure used for checking the students' homework.
4. Make suggestions for improvement:
   a. How might you improve the content of the homework?
   b. Is spiraling evident? If not, how might you include questions from past areas of study that might be helpful for the students to review?
   c. Is the quantity of problems appropriate? For example, are there too many of the same type of problem assigned?
5. Comment on the effectiveness and efficiency of the procedures for the review and assessment of students' homework, and give suggestions for improvement.
6. Based on what you have observed about the homework process, make conjectures regarding the teacher's goals for students, beliefs about the purpose of homework and how students learn best, and knowledge of the students, content, and methods of pedagogy.
7. Interview the teacher regarding homework policies that may not be observable to you. For example, find out how the teacher creates the homework assignments, and whether the teacher ever assigns projects to students.

Observation Example

In his observation report, Keith showed an awareness that, based on the nature of the homework assignment, the teacher he was observing did not expect enough of her students:

> [The teacher's] current homework assignment as well as the past lesson's homework was much too easy. I can tell by the number of chorus responses by the class that the class seemed bored and unenthused. For example, the previous lesson was on graphing parabolas. The homework consisted of a few very easy questions where the students were asked to move the parabola along the y-axis according to the equation shown.

Keith used the discourse to ascertain that the assignment was far too easy. By so doing, he showed his awareness of the close link that exists between tasks and discourse.

Keith also gave a good suggestion for improvement:

> So much more could have been done. For example, she could have produced examples of leading coefficients with a negative sign that would

change the concavity of the parabola. The children could have been challenged a lot more. They could have made discoveries about what happens when you change the coefficients and this would have motivated them more for the upcoming lesson.

Judging from the nature of her assignment, Keith decided that, "The teacher used the homework assignment as a review of previous material learned." From the suggestion he gave for improving the assignment, it appears that Keith saw the potential for homework being used as an opportunity for students to make discoveries that can lead to a motivation for learning the next lesson. He also noticed the missed opportunity to use homework as a review of material learned in the past. He said, "Spiraling was not evident in this assignment. It was too bad, since that could have been used to review throughout the semester rather than only before an exam." Keith also found fault with the procedure the teacher used to review the homework:

> The teacher went over the homework directly after the Do Now was presented at the beginning of the lesson. She selected a few homework questions to be put on the board and had the children (selected randomly) put up their answers. Although this seemed like a good tactic at first, it defeated its own purpose later on in that the teacher controlled most of the discussion. The students did not explain their work to the rest of the class. The teacher answered most of the questions that came from the classmates. The children should be able to reason and communicate mathematically, and this would have been a great opportunity to allow students to obtain confidence in math. Overall, the review was clear and concise and only lasted about 5 to 10 minutes. The only problem was that the teacher did not empower the students who attempted to do the homework problems.

Keith recognized the importance of giving students a more active role in the homework review. He then went on to describe the teacher's assessment procedure:

> She checked the homework by walking around the room during the Do Now portion of the class. I noticed she was very strict when it came to writing down the questions before writing an answer. She also insisted that the students frame their answers by either drawing a box around it or underlining the correct response.

Although Keith agreed with the teacher's insistence on proper form, he noticed again the teacher's disinterest in seeing students' thought processes:

> I strongly agree with the teacher's insistence on good format. Homework needs to be a tool for the student to use for review after completion, so neatness and clarity are important. However, I think the teacher should have placed a greater emphasis on noticing the quality of the mathematical work the students produced.

Underlying Keith's comments is his awareness that if the teacher does not assess the quality of the students' mathematical work, she cannot monitor student understanding and thus cannot regulate the instruction appropriately.

Based on the homework procedures of this teacher, Keith was able to make conjectures about her view of homework, her beliefs about her role as a teacher, and her knowledge of the students:

> I think that this teacher thinks that homework is to be used for review of problems exactly like those learned in the previous day's lesson. I don't think this teacher really knows the ability of her students because she never asks them to explain their work at the board or answer other students' questions. Also, when she checks homework, she mainly looks at format and doesn't really study the mathematical thinking of the students. The problems are so simple that it leads me to believe that she doesn't think her students are capable of thinking beyond what she has shown them. I think she believes that her role is to show students exactly how to do certain problems and then to make sure that they do it exactly the way she has shown them.

Keith understood that without giving students the opportunity to explain themselves, teachers can never increase their knowledge of the understanding and abilities of their students.

The next observation assignment concerns an essential part of every mathematics class—the use of class time. The use of class time throughout the full period involves a discussion of lesson phases as well as all dimensions of instructional practice: tasks, learning environment, and discourse.

OBSERVATION 5: USE OF CLASS TIME (PHASES, TASKS, LEARNING ENVIRONMENT, DISCOURSE)

Instructional time is very precious in the secondary school setting. One of the main complaints of teachers is that they don't have enough time to work with the students. This is especially true in schools that only have periods that have from 40 to 50 minutes of instructional time per day. It is therefore essential that teachers use their precious class time effectively and efficiently. To accomplish this, teachers must create a learning environment in which students cooperate with the teacher and with one another. Furthermore, teachers must create tasks that engage the students from the moment they enter the room to the moment they leave. Teachers also must orchestrate task-oriented, productive discourse. Finally, the phases of the lesson must allow for introduction, development, and closure to ideas. The way teachers make use of the limited time they have is largely an outgrowth of the priorities they have which are a reflection of their cognitions.

Observation Procedure

A first step in learning how to take maximum advantage of limited classroom time is to observe how others make use of their time. The purpose of this observation is to make you aware of and sensitive to how each minute of class time is used in the class that you observe.

1. Use a watch to keep track of how every minute is used in the class that you observe. Record what the teacher and the students are doing during each time interval.
2. Make note of the instructional strategies that are used and indicate in which phases of the lesson they occur.
3. Create a lesson plan that you think best fits the lesson. In your plan, identify the teacher's main objectives for the lesson and decide whether his or her instructional strategies and use of time were supportive of accomplishing the goals.
4. Be sensitive to the teacher's movement, or lack of movement, in the room and the effects generated by the teacher's position.
5. Identify the existence of lesson phases and describe how the tasks, learning environment, and discourse affected the use of class time in the lesson.
6. Make conjectures regarding the teacher's goals, knowledge, and beliefs.

Observation Example

In the class that Joshua observed, students had taken an exam the day before, and the teacher focused the lesson on the types of problems that students found difficult. Joshua documented the time frames of this review lesson that incorporated the use of cooperative learning. It was a 45–minute lesson. During the first 6 minutes, students worked individually on two problems. During the next 4 minutes, students were divided into groups and given an assignment, followed by the next 18 minutes in which they worked in groups, and the next 12 minutes in which different students explained portions of the group work to the class. The teacher used the final 5 minutes to return test papers and assign homework. Joshua noted the way the teacher monitored and regulated the instruction during the group work section: "The groups worked well together, but they began to lose their focus after about 14 minutes. The teacher began to notice that the room was getting unruly, so he ended the group session and had the students return their desks to their normal position. I felt that the session lasted about 5 minutes too long, but I had the luxury of being an observer in the class and was not busy helping the students as the teacher was." Joshua recognized the different perspectives one has as a teacher of a lesson versus an observer of a lesson and that careful orchestration of a lesson can be very tricky.

Joshua explained the teacher's instructional strategy as follows: "The main instructional strategy used was cooperative learning. The teacher had students go to the blackboard, do the problem and explain their work. The students explained the work to the teacher and the class as they wrote it on the board."

Joshua had a positive impression of the teacher's movement during the class: "The teacher was away from the board for the cooperative learning session. He moved around quite a bit and talked to each group. Before and after the group session, the teacher remained at the front of the room. All of the students were working during the group session. . . . I think the students genuinely enjoyed having the teacher move around the room and work with them in small groups. It seemed to energize them through the rest of the class." Joshua saw the value of using diverse instructional strategies during the course of one lesson and the importance of the timing of these instructional strategies. That is, for this particular class, had the teacher allowed the students to work in small groups during the entire period, it would not have been effective.

Even though this was a review lesson, Joshua noticed the phases that existed during this lesson:

> At the start of the class, the teacher introduced the two types of problems that the students had trouble with on the previous day's test: algebraic fractions with division and the other subtraction with unlike denominators. He gave them different types of problems to do in the groups and asked them to notice the patterns. This was like the development of the lesson. At the end of the class, he had several students summarize how to do the two types of problems introduced at the beginning. This was the closure of the lesson.

Joshua made interesting conjectures regarding the teacher's beliefs about how students learn: "The fact that this teacher allotted 18 minutes for students to work on the problems in groups and 12 minutes for students to explain their work to the class tells me that he believes in the value of having students learn from one another and communicate their ideas. He didn't feel that he had to explain it himself to get the students to understand it." Joshua made the connection between a teacher's beliefs and how he apportioned the time in his class.

The next observation assignment concerns the verbal behavior of individual students throughout the class period. No discussion of verbal behavior can take place without discussing the discourse that occurs within the class.

OBSERVATION 6: VERBAL BEHAVIOR
OF INDIVIDUAL STUDENTS (DISCOURSE)

The value of having students communicate mathematically is undisputed today. The vision of an effective mathematics class is no longer one in which the teacher is talking and the students are quietly taking notes and doing problems at their seats. In the mathematics class of the 21st century, students are expected to actively participate in their learning. They are expected to express themselves verbally. That is, they should be engaged in a verbal exchange of mathematical concepts with their teacher and with their classmates. Although having every student in the class engaged in conversation about mathematics during some segment of the class time is an admirable goal, it is very difficult to accomplish. In most classes, some students do not speak at all, others monopolize the class discussion, and others veer away from the subject matter. In most cases, the teacher bears the responsibility for the nature of the verbal interactions that occur in the class. For example, if the teacher designs a well-structured cooperative learning activity, the probability will be high that each student will have the opportunity to speak about mathematics. If the teacher only calls on students who raise their hands, probably only a small segment of the class will verbally express their mathematical ideas. If the teacher does not design interesting tasks and has not created a productive and respectful learning environment, chances are the students will be talking to each other about topics other than mathematics.

It is clear then that the verbal interactions are largely dependent on the tasks teachers' design, the learning environment they create, and the discourse they promote. Therefore, it seems reasonable to assume that teachers' cognitions (goals, knowledge and beliefs) play a critical role in the verbal interactions that occur within a class. For example, a teacher who believes that it is essential to have all students explain their mathematical reasoning aloud and has the knowledge of instructional strategies that will engage all students in verbal mathematical communication will not just call on a select group of students but will give all of the students a chance to participate in the discussion. It is important for you to become sensitive to the verbal interactions that occur during class so that when you teach, you will be more aware of the discourse that occurs within your class.

Observation Procedure

Observation 6 includes the following steps:

1. Make a rough seating chart, and indicate with an appropriate arrow each time a student speaks. There are a variety of arrows indicating different types of verbal interaction (see Appendix B-6 for a legend for verbal flow and Appendix C-1 for a sample verbal interaction chart):
   a. Three different types of arrows facing up indicate that a student volunteered a verbal expression (gave a correct response, gave an irrelevant or incorrect response, asked a question about the content).
   b. Two different types of arrows facing downward indicate that a student was called on by the teacher and responded either correctly or incorrectly.

     c. Other arrows indicate that students talked to one another about the subject matter, or that they talked to one another about non-subject matters.

     d. Another symbol indicates that the teacher conferred with a student.

2. Analyze the verbal flow within the class.

     a. Examine any patterns of verbal behavior based on seating position, achievement, gender, race, ethnicity, language, and personality.

     b. Report on who spoke and who didn't, who gave correct responses, and who gave irrelevant responses, who got called on and who did not, which students spoke together about the subject and which spoke off the subject. Did any students dominate the discussion?

3. Determine how the patterns of verbal behavior are related to the tasks, learning environment, and questioning style of the teacher.

4. Make conjectures regarding the teacher's goals for the students in this particular lesson, the teacher's knowledge of the students in this class, and the teacher's beliefs about specific students or groups of students and their ability to learn mathematics.

Observation Examples

Elena observed a class in which there was very little verbal behavior regarding the subject matter and too much regarding nonsubject matter. Elena detected the relationship between the teacher's poor questioning style and the lack of subject-directed verbal behavior of the students:

> A total of only 12 students (40 percent) participated during the lesson. The teacher could increase this percentage by calling on particular students for responses, especially those who are not paying attention or do not participate at all. Besides, the class management should be less teacher-centered. The few questions the teacher actually asked were directed to the whole class. Students' responses were choral responses. The teacher should let students come up with their own explanations instead of him explaining all the exercises.

Elena also noted how the teacher-dominated approach used in this lesson contributed to verbal interactions that were not related to the subject:

> The right side of the classroom was involved in having irrelevant conversations. Students were talking about the color of a lipstick or about a

party coming up this Saturday. They raised their hands to ask irrelevant questions such as whether they could go to the bathroom or not. This happened because the teacher talked for the whole period of class, and he did not let students participate. He did not use any challenging problems so students could be more interested in the lesson. He did not move from the board, and he completely ignored students who were not paying attention to his lecture.

Elena had an interesting conjecture regarding this teacher's knowledge of his students: "I believe that this teacher knows his students, and he knows who is doing well and who is repeating. However, I do not understand why he does not realize how boring a repeating lesson could be for some of his students." Elena raises an interesting question with regard to what is in the mind of this teacher. If he knows his students' abilities and past experiences, why isn't he tailoring his instruction to meet the needs of these students? Does he lack knowledge of ways to make it interesting, or doesn't he believe it is his responsibility to make it interesting? The important thing about this observation is that it caused Elena to make the link between the students' verbal behaviors and the cognitions of the teacher.

An interesting observation report written by Wenling, a student teacher who had recently emigrated from China, described a pattern of verbal behavior of high-achieving Asian students:

> There were differences between talkers and nontalkers, not only by gender but also by race and seating pattern. The data told me that Asian students were generally quiet in contrast to the second biggest population they occupied in the class. I believe that culture and motivation were two major factors that were preventing many Asian children from being verbally active. I grew up in China. When I was younger, I was taught not to talk too much. My parents, my teachers, and the society did not promote free speech. Older people always told the younger ones that society would not judge a person by his way of talking but by his intelligence that would only show on his work. Furthermore, Chinese people believed "less talk, less trouble." I always believe that whites are generally free with speech.

Wenling made conjectures regarding the teacher's knowledge and beliefs about the problem with Asian students and their lack of verbal participation:

I think this teacher knows that Asian students are mostly quiet and don't feel comfortable saying anything in the class. I think she believes that it is best to leave them alone so they would not be embarrassed. But I think that is a shame since it would be good for them to learn to speak up in class. As a future teacher, I have to learn to help diverse students to achieve the goal of speaking mathematics fluently. Indeed, some verbal behaviors can be changed when sufficient training is given. Communicating mathematics is definitely one of the important skills that all of our children should be capable of.

Wenling also noticed the relationship between the difficulty level of the tasks and the verbal behavior of the students:

The truth was that many quiet students were really advanced and they already knew the material. The lesson was not challenging and interesting to them. They were totally bored by it. I felt there was not enough enrichment material or activity for these talents. For example, one Asian girl who sat next to me sighed many times. She looked like she did not want to be in the class any more. Yet, she was the only one who could answer the tough questions when everyone else was stuck.

Wenling also noticed that unchallenging tasks caused some students to talk about subjects other than mathematics:

I noticed that when the white students got bored, they talked to their neighbors who had something in common with them. Some children enjoyed making fun of each other. Some children talked to each other because they wanted to hear the events that happened earlier. All this tells me that each lesson plan has to be very interesting in order to motivate every student to learn. To prevent students from talking about irrelevant matters during a lesson is a critical task. It is not an easy job.

The next observation assignment concerns the task orientation of individual students throughout the class period. All three dimensions of instructional practice have a direct effect on the task orientation of students: tasks, learning environment, and discourse.

OBSERVATION 7: TASK ORIENTATION OF INDIVIDUAL STUDENTS (TASKS, LEARNING ENVIRONMENT, DISCOURSE)

One of the critical concerns of beginning teachers is how to maintain discipline in their classes. The idea of losing control of adolescent students can be very frightening, especially for recent college graduates who are often not much older than their students. While discipline can be a great challenge in certain types of classes, the best prevention against such problems is to create well-designed tasks, a respectful learning environment, and active discourse during all phases of the lesson. A first step in learning how to do this is to observe firsthand the connection between the on-task and off-task behaviors of students and the dimensions of a lesson throughout each phase of the lesson.

Observation Procedure

Observation 7 includes the following steps:

Keep track of the on-task and off-task behaviors of each of the students throughout all phases of the lesson. This is done by systematically observing each student in the class and recording his or her task behavior at each interval of time throughout the class period.

1. Make a line graph in which the vertical axis consists of the number of students who are on task and the horizontal axis consists of the time intervals in which the behaviors were observed. This line graph provides a picture of the on-task behaviors that occurred throughout all phases of the lesson. (Most student teachers predict that the line graph of a typical class will be a normal curve. That is, when students first enter the class, very few will be on task. As the period progresses, more and more students will become involved, arriving at a maximum level of on-task behavior by the middle of the class. Then our students predict that there will be a steady drop off in student attention by the end of the class and again, very few will be on task. Surprisingly, only a few graphs turn out to look like the normal curve.)

2. Describe the data by reporting how many students were in the class and what percentage of students were working as the teacher expected during different phases of the lesson.

3. Report the times at which the on-task behaviors were at their maximum and minimum levels.

4. Analyze the relationship between the levels of on-task behaviors you observed and the specific tasks that were assigned, the learning environment that existed, and the type of discourse that was in place during those particular time periods.

5. Give suggestions for improving the percentage of on-task behaviors.

6. Make conjectures regarding the teacher's goals, knowledge of students and pedagogy, and beliefs regarding his or her role in keeping students on task during the lesson.

7. Compare the results of your previous observation with this present observation (both done of the same class) to notice whether there are any relationships between the students' verbal behaviors and task orientations.

Observation Examples

This section includes observations done by several student teachers. In the first observation, Lena noticed the critical relationship of the timing of a task and how long students maintain their interest. Her line graph, which appears in Appendix C-2, dipped and rose during the beginning of the class.

> The first task was group work so this lent itself to allow for some off-task interaction. We can see from the line graph that after 10 minutes, the at task percentage dropped from 84% to only 48%. This shows us the importance of time constraints on even the most interesting of tasks. Once students are done or become bored, they start behaving off task, which, when students are working in groups, will more than likely spread to their partners.

> We can also see from the graph that immediately following this drop in participation, the teacher switched tasks, bringing the entire class population to full attention. This task happened to involve new material, so it held the class' attention for a significant amount of time. Yet as with all tasks, once they run too long, attention begins to drop again, as we can verify from the line graph. The 100% on task eventually dropped to 72%. From this I would suggest that time limits on each task and variation of tasks may help to keep the largest number of students on task the longest.

Dorothy, noticed that quiet students were not necessarily students who are on task. She also recognized the need to time the activities properly and, more importantly, to monitor the students closely to determine the proper timing. (See Appendix C-3 for the graph.)

> The teacher that I observed has excellent control over the volume of her classes. Her students are virtually silent, and that seems to be the way she likes them. However, in doing this observation, I could see that a silent classroom does not mean that the students are all on task.
>
> The class that I observed had 20 students. At the start of the period, about 55% of the students were on task. However, the teacher left too much time for the student to do their Do Now. This caused many of the students to lose interest and come of task. This can be seen on the graph between 11:40 and 11:45 a.m., where the students were least attentive; only three students were on task (15%). When the teacher started to go over the Do Now at 11:50 (already 20 minutes after the period had started) most of the students (95%) were on task.
>
> Even when the students were off task they remained silent. During the first twenty minutes of class the teacher was sitting at her desk, grading tests from another class. This should not have been done during class time. Had the teacher gotten out from behind her desk and walked around the classroom, she would have noticed that most of the students were finished with the Do Now and were sitting and daydreaming, or working on homework from other classes.

Dorothy also noticed the relationship between the verbal interactions she noted in the previous observation and the task behaviors she noted in this observation. She recognized how the teacher's questioning style affected the learning environment, the level of task engagement, and ultimately what they learned:

> When I observed this class for Observation 6, I noticed that this teacher seemed to have very little interaction with her students. I have never seen her call on any particular student by name. When she asks questions to the class, she simply waits for some faceless voice to call out the answer. The entire classroom environment is very cold and impersonal. The fact that the students sit by in silent protest (as opposed to acting out by talking, etc.) adds to the already eerie setting. The students seem almost like robots; they carry out their task and then sit silently. I don't

know what they are learning, but I can't imagine any concepts to be understood on a deeper level with so little participation of the students.

When it came to her thoughts on the teacher's knowledge of the students and pedagogy, Dorothy seemed confused:

It is hard for me to judge this teacher's knowledge of pedagogy based on what I saw. I don't know whether she teaches this way because she doesn't know any better or because she just doesn't care. Maybe she believes that as a teacher she shouldn't have to take any work home with her and so she thinks it is OK to get her work done during class time. Or does she really believe that it is not her job to give students individual attention? I can't imagine that teaching in the way she does, she knows very much about her individual students.

Even though Dorothy is confused, she understands that there is a distinct connection between this teacher's beliefs and the low level of student participation in the class.

The next observation assignment concerns the assessment procedures used with the class. A discussion of methods of assessment is clearly a discussion of methods of monitoring and regulation.

OBSERVATION 8: ASSESSMENT (MONITORING AND REGULATING)

One of the main purposes of assessment is to help teachers better understand what students know and do not know and make meaningful instructional decisions based on that information. Within our model, this would primarily fall under the category of monitoring and regulating. Beginning teachers often think that assessment is synonymous with testing. This common misconception could not be further from the truth. Assessment is an ongoing process that takes place within classrooms every day as students and teachers interact. The fact that it is usually undocumented information should not detract from appreciating its importance. Ongoing student assessment is the teacher's main problem-solving technique—the problem being to help students learn mathematics. By monitoring student understanding and regulating the instruction based on the feedback obtained, teachers can maximize their chances of helping students learn.

In short, assessment of student understanding must be an integral part of instruction.

Teaching has been recognized as a profession in which decisions are made every few seconds. That means teachers must be flexible, able to change the path of their lesson based on their assessment of the students. Teachers frequently walk out of their classrooms feeling defeated because they were not able to "cover the material." While it is important to adhere to a syllabus, we believe that teachers who cover the curriculum without regard to whether students are "with them" are making a big mistake. This kind of teaching is based on a belief that a teacher's number one role is to complete the curriculum, and student understanding is a distant second. We often tell student teachers, "If you could teach the same lesson with or without the students in the room, then something is radically wrong." The marks of an effective teacher are knowledge and flexibility to change the course of a lesson based on an assessment of student understanding. This on-the-spot decision making is very difficult for beginning teachers for two reasons. First, they are so concentrated on following their plan and what they are doing that they fail to recognize whether or not the students understand the work. Second, if they do recognize that the students are confused, they are at a loss for how to help them and are threatened by the thought of not following their preplanned script. Knowing how to change directions in a lesson takes expertise that usually takes years of experience to develop.

Assessment strategies are not only used to help teachers adjust their instruction. They are used as the basis for evaluation. That is, a part of every teacher's job is to assign some sort of a grade to represent the students' levels of understanding. How teachers formulate their grades is a reflection of what they value. For example, a teacher who thinks that it is important for students to be able to verbally communicate and defend their mathematical ideas will probably count class participation as part of their grade.

Observation 8 is designed to make you aware of assessment opportunities that can occur during a class session, ways teachers can alter their instruction based on the feedback they receive from students, and techniques teachers can use to assess student understanding as well as the criteria they use to evaluate students.

Observation Procedure

Observation 8 is divided into two parts.

1. Examine the questioning and responses of both teachers and students. When a teacher asks a question, what is he or she trying to assess? When the student responds to the question, what is the assessment of student understanding that the teacher can make? How does the teacher use the feedback obtained from student responses? When a student asks a question, what evaluative judgment can the teacher make? How does the teacher use that feedback to improve instruction?

   a. Try to find at least five examples of ongoing assessment and regulation of instruction.
   b. Record any episodes of discourse that reveal how a teacher assessed student understanding during instruction and show how the teacher used this assessment to alter the instruction.
   c. Record any opportunities that you feel the teacher missed. Were there times that the students said or did something that indicated that a change in the course of the lesson was necessary? What were you able to assess about the students' level of understanding that would suggest such a change was necessary? What type of change would you suggest?
   d. Guess what the teacher's knowledge and beliefs are about mathematical pedagogy. Does the teacher believe it is important to monitor student understanding during the course of instruction? Does the teacher think it is important to change the course of the lesson based on student input? If so, does the teacher know how to adjust the level of instruction to meet the needs of the students?
   e. Make conjectures regarding the teacher's goals.

2. Interview a teacher regarding his or her formal assessment strategies and the methods used to evaluate students, and make a conjecture regarding this teacher's goals for his or her students. What does this teacher believe is of value for students to know, to believe, and be able to do?

Observation Examples

Danielle recognized the connection between student questioning and ongoing assessment:

> I found very good ongoing assessment and a high rate of class participation—something that is vital to good ongoing classroom assessment. I also found that the teacher did a pretty good job of questioning any answer a student gave—whether it was right or not—so that the students' confidence in their answers would have to be based only on how

much mathematical sense it made to them, and not on how the teacher was reacting to the answer. This way the teacher can assess better whether the student really knows what they are doing, or if they are just taking a shot in the dark, and either sticking to it or changing their minds depending on the teacher's reaction.

Danielle also gave a good example of how a teacher regulated her instruction based on her assessment of student understanding:

When one student wanted to take $(\tan x + \sin 2x)/\tan x$, and just cancel both $\tan x$ to get $\sin 2x$, she decided to take a couple of minutes to show why that doesn't work, especially because before, another student had taken $(\tan x \times \sin 2x)/\tan x$ and canceled both $\tan x$ and had not understood why he couldn't do it. Since no student was able to explain it better than to say "Because you just can't," she decided it was important to show them. She demonstrated it with the examples $(8 + 4)/24$ and $(8 \times 4)/24$, which students could see more clearly. This was an example of using ongoing assessment to adjust a lesson plan according to the needs of the class. Not only that, but the fact that she first went to another student to answer a student's question, rather than at first answering it herself, shows that even one student's question is utilized for the assessment of the other students.

Danielle has demonstrated how this teacher's knowledge of content pedagogy allowed her to give the students an on-the-spot problem that would clarify the confusion.

Danielle pointed out that to be able to assess all of the students during class, the teacher should have called on all the students, which she did not do. Danielle gave a reasonable suggestion for involving all of the students:

There were at least two students whose mouths didn't open even once the whole period, and probably four or five who were noticeably much less involved than the others. I think part of her wanting to keep the atmosphere nonthreatening goes a little too far—by just engaging students who may feel uncomfortable with being called on. The loss is that these students do not have the opportunity to demonstrate their knowledge through any avenue other than the tests. I think that if she thought of ways to gradually and gently bring these students into the conversation—ask them very simple things at first, for example—she may get the feeling that they are more willing to participate, and call on them more often, so that she can assess them in the classroom as well, rather than having to leave it completely up to her imagination whether or not they are following.

Danielle made some interesting conjectures regarding the goals, knowledge, and beliefs of this teacher:

> Judging from how the teacher insists that students use the correct mathematical language and how she questions them all the time, I can tell that she thinks it is important for them to communicate their thoughts and she really is interested in knowing what is in their minds. She was also very flexible about digressing from the lesson to make sure students understood a concept. The examples she gave really cleared up the concept and showed that she had good pedagogical knowledge.

Another student, George gave this argument for using cooperative learning to improve the accuracy of one teacher's assessment of her students: "If the class had some cooperative group time, the teacher could have strolled around the room and listened in on students' conversations with each other. An adolescent would probably be more relaxed in a conversation with another adolescent than with an authority figure such as a teacher. By listening in on this kind of conversation, a teacher can gain insights and assessments that she couldn't get otherwise."

Edna was pleased to interview a teacher who used some nontraditional formal assessment and evaluation strategies:

> The teacher has a simple formula for formulating grades. Students' class participation is one essential consideration. For every single student, she keeps an index card and at the end of each day, she jots down any students that had very good participation, or poor behavior. When calculating grades, she looks at these index cards, along with tests, logs (the students in all of her classes keep daily logs) and portfolios. She does not weigh each item evenly. For example, for the research class I observed, she counted the portfolios and participation much more heavily than the two tests they had taken.

Edna was impressed that the teacher documented students' daily participation. Such a technique not only enables the teacher to remember the incidences of participation more accurately, but it demonstrates that the teacher genuinely values what students say during classroom instruction.

Although Edna was impressed with this teacher's method of evaluation, she expressed some concerns: "I felt this method of evaluation was very thorough. The only problem that I see in it is that it's somewhat difficult, and students generally prefer a more precise formula in order to figure out their grades. Additionally, I don't think it's objective enough." Edna is already sensitive to the issue of objectivity, which is a source of discussion today as teachers consider alternative forms of assessment. It is good that. Edna recognized that this teacher's goals for student learning went far beyond being able to understand how to solve certain problems:

> Obviously, this teacher placed a high value on having the students be able to explain mathematics both verbally and in written form. From the way this teacher spoke to me in the interview, and judging from the fact that in her research class she counted her students' participation and portfolios more than their test grades, tells me that she wants these students to appreciate mathematics and feel confident in their ability to express themselves.

Edna has made the connection between the grading policy of the teacher and the goals the teacher has for the students.

These examples show that ongoing monitoring of students occurs in many ways through many sources. The teacher's ability to regulate instruction to meet the needs of the students is a critical aspect of teaching for student understanding. Therefore, it is important that teachers not only monitor the feedback they get from students but also have accurate and equitable underlying assumptions of students' needs, interests, and abilities.

The next observation assignment concerns the preexisting impressions and expectations teachers may have about different students or groups of students and how they are reflected in the discourse that occurs within their classes and the tasks students are assigned.

OBSERVATION 9: TEACHER EXPECTATIONS AND STEREOTYPING (DISCOURSE, TASKS)

The reform movement stresses the need for all students to learn mathematics—with particular emphasis on the word *all*. It is no longer acceptable for mathematical understanding to be accessible to mainly white males. Students of all races, ethnicity, socioeconomic levels, physical conditions, religions, languages, and genders must have equal opportunities to learn mathematics. Most teachers would dispute the allegation that they allow stereotyping to interfere with their ability to offer equal opportunities to all their mathematics students. But teachers' deep-rooted beliefs about the abilities of different groups of students cannot help but be reflected in their discourse with students.

For example, teachers communicate their expectations of student performance by how they respond when students have trouble with a task. Teachers who believe students are capable of carrying out tasks will suggest ideas for how to do it, thus enabling the students to succeed on their own. Teachers who believe students cannot carry out tasks will perform them for the students. When teachers do tasks for their students, the students conclude that their teachers do not believe that they are capable of performing the tasks themselves. In time, students come to share the expectations of their teachers.

Another way that teachers communicate their expectations of student performance is through the length of wait time they use. There are two kinds of wait times in a classroom. The first is the time between asking a question and calling on a student, which teachers should extend to give all students an opportunity to think about an answer in preparation for being called on. We have already dealt with this type of wait time in a previous observation. The second kind is the wait time between calling on a student and achieving some kind of resolution—receiving the answer, rephrasing the question, or moving on to another student for the answer. Research shows that teachers tend to wait longer for students from whom they expect correct answers. They tend to wait longer for interpretative and opinion answers than for factual answers. They tend to wait longer for answers from boys in math and science classes, and longer for answers from girls in English classes. The significance of long wait times, then, is that it signals to students that you have confidence in their ability to answer questions, which in turn motivates students to try harder to offer answers and thus to succeed.

A third way that teachers communicate their expectations of student performance is through the feedback they give to students regarding their academic performance. Although many teachers realize the instructive benefits of praising and correcting students on their written work, they are unaware and less conscious of the verbal feedback they give to students in the classroom. For example, gender studies have revealed that boys receive more feedback from teachers than girls do. Boys are both praised more for right answers and criticized more for wrong ones than girls are. One researcher even found sex-stereotyped variations on the type of feedback, with boys encouraged to try harder when they answer a question wrong but girls are praised for trying (Campbell, 1995; Oakes, 1990; Secada, 1992).

When students feel that their answers receive little response from their teachers, they have less reason to work hard. These are the students who learn less and are more likely to discontinue their mathematics studies as soon as they have the opportunity. This observation is designed to sensitize you to subtle evidence of bias in the classroom and to heighten your awareness of how beliefs about students can directly shape the nature of the discourse within the classroom.

Observation Procedure

Observation 9 has two parts. The first part includes the following steps:

1. Make a seating chart of the class, indicating any observable characteristics of each of the students (e.g., gender, race/ethnicity, handicapping conditions).
2. Keep track of the discourse that occurs between the teacher and the individual students by indicating the following:
   a. Whether the wait time is less than or greater than 5 seconds.
   b. Whether the teacher accepts, praises, corrects, criticizes, or rejects a student's answer.
   c. Whether the teacher shows the student how to do a problem or gives the student a hint how to do the problem.
3. Look for patterns of discourse that occur with any specific groups of students.
4. Make a conjecture regarding this teacher's beliefs about the abilities of certain groups of students.

The second part of this observation includes these steps:

1. Notice whether there are any signs of stereotyping in the tasks students are assigned or in the classroom or school environment.
2. Carefully observe assigned problems, posters, bulletin boards, and other materials visible in the mathematics classrooms or hallways of the school to see how people are represented. For example, are the tasks geared towards male interests? How many women and how many men are pic-

tured? How many people of different races or ethnicity pictured? What are they doing? How are they described? Do these representations reveal any stereotyping? What do they say about the beliefs of society in general?

Observation Examples

Nicky noticed evidence of gender bias in the way the teacher that she observed conducted the discourse:

> In this class, there were 20 girls and 13 boys. Whenever the teacher called on a girl to answer a question, he waited less than 5 seconds and then proceeded to explain the answer and the procedure for how to get the answer. In one instance, he called on a female student, and while she was answering the question, he proceeded to answer the question and drown out the girl's voice. I might add, from previous observations I noticed this girl never speaks in this class and now I understand why. On the other hand, when a male member of the class answered a question, he allowed the student to answer.

Nicky had strong feelings about the probable beliefs of this teacher regarding differential abilities of males and females. She said: "I really think that this teacher doesn't have much confidence in the ability of his female students. He doesn't seem to want to waste time waiting for them to answer a question, and when they do try to answer a question, he cuts them off. I think he assumes they won't give the correct answer and if they do, they won't be able to explain it."

This observation assignment enabled Nicky, who was given the opportunity to teach a class of her own in the school, to become aware of her own biases: "This observation has made me aware of a few of my own gender biases. I have noticed that I tend to pay less attention to the female students because of the behavioral problems I have with the male students in the classroom. In this manner, my female students suffer from not getting as much attention that they deserve."

Rehana noticed differential treatment of males with respect to discipline as well:

> The one time that I saw the teacher show bias against a boy was while she was walking around the room. A boy across the room was turned

around in his chair and was talking to the girl behind him. The teacher yelled at him and told him to turn around. A few minutes later the boy and girl were talking again, but he was talking while facing forward. The teacher heard and threatened him with detention. My problem was that both the boy and girl were talking and she didn't once yell at the girl.

Although the issue of discipline was not addressed in the original assignment, Nicky's and Rehana's findings precipitated an interesting class discussion regarding the effects of negative attention and how it might actually be encouraging the boys to misbehave.

Boris noted bias in the posters he observed in the school: "As for famous mathematicians, most of them pictured were of white men." Boris credited this problem with lack of knowledge on the part of the teachers: "I don't think that the reason the posters were all of white men was because the teachers were biased against females or other races. I think they are just not aware of the work done by females and people from other ethnic groups and the posters of these people are not that available. This may point to historian's bias but I'm not sure."

Mitch taught in a school that was sensitive to issues of equity. He noticed evidence of equity in the textbooks and posters:

The newer math textbooks they used pictured as many, if not more, females engaged in mathematical activities than males. I found a math bulletin board with two very interesting printed posters. One pictured a woven rug and had an inset with a Navajo woman weaving one of them; the text mentioned the intricate geometric concepts and relationships inherent in the designs of these rugs. It highlighted intuitive mental math and visualization skills exhibited in these hand woven crafts by the Navajo women. There was a second poster depicting a system of calculation used in India centuries ago.

Although one might object to the stereotype of women sewing rather than "doing math," the important thing is that Mitch was sensitive to the representation of mathematical ideas being credited to people other than white males.

The last observation assignment is a culminating activity that gives you the chance to integrate the ideas you have learned from the previous nine observations.

OBSERVATION 10: CULMINATING OBSERVATION

By the time you do this observation assignment you will have already observed teachers' instructional practice from many vantage points. In the previous nine observation assignments, you noted different aspects of teachers' instructional practice and made conjectures about the underlying teacher cognitions that may have accounted for what you observed. You critiqued the tasks, learning environment, and discourse, as well as the teacher's use of phases and monitoring and regulating of instruction. Based on this information, you then considered what the teachers' goals, knowledge, and beliefs were. At this point, you are ready to put all the pieces of the puzzle together and observe all the dimensions of teaching at one time.

Observation Procedure

The first part of this observation includes the following steps:

1. Observe and critique all aspects of instruction in one lesson and make conjectures regarding all aspects of the teacher's cognition.
2. Organize your assessment according to the nine categories from the (PDF) framework (see Table 1), incorporating all the variables you have been sensitized to in your previous nine observations. The categories are grouped according to the dimensions of teaching.
   a. Under the dimension of tasks, the categories are *modes of representation, motivational strategies,* and *sequencing/difficulty level.*
   b. Under the dimension of learning environment, the categories are *social/intellectual climate, modes of instruction/pacing,* and *administrative routines.*
   c. Under the dimension of discourse, the categories are *teacher-student interaction, student-student interaction,* and *questioning.*

The second part of this observation involves making conjectures regarding the cognitions of the teacher during the three stages of teaching:

1. During the preactive stage, make conjectures about the teacher's overarching cognitions: goals, knowledge of pupils, knowledge of content, knowledge of pedagogy, beliefs about the students' role in instruction, beliefs about the content, beliefs about the teacher's role in instruction.
2. During the interactive stage, make conjectures about the nature of the teacher's monitoring and regulating during instruction.

3. To assess the teacher's postactive cognitions—self-assessing and reflecting— interview the teacher following the lesson, if possible.

Observation Example

Maria was quite critical of the lesson she observed. It was apparent that she was sensitive to the weaknesses of the lesson that existed within every category. For example, within the category modes of representation, Maria explained that to clarify the distinction between nested triangles, the teacher should have either used different colored chalk or an overhead projector. Maria was disappointed that the only motivation used was extrinsic, that is, the threat of the Regents exam. It was a review lesson, so she took no issue with the sequencing or difficulty level.

As for the social/intellectual climate of the class, Maria was convinced that it was poor and gave good reasons for feeling so: "The students clearly do not like this teacher, do not feel he cares about them, and do not feel he respects their intelligence or thoughts. This is clear from some of the comments students said to me after class, and from the way he treats them during class." Maria criticized the teacher's pacing because he never let students explain their ideas and "right or wrong" would just "move on." Although she thought his administrative routines were good in that "students settled in quickly," she had an idea to improve the procedure by writing the problems on a transparency which would save time from having to write them on the board.

Maria had major criticisms of the discourse. Regarding teacher-student interaction, she said, "It was terrible! The teacher showed no respect for anything that any student said. He gave no positive feedback for either correct or incorrect answers, never asked how a student got an answer— showing that he really didn't care how their minds worked, but only what their mouths said." Notice how Maria is able to relate the teacher's instructional practice with the teacher's thoughts. Regarding student-student interaction, Maria said, "There was basically none. No student was asked to comment on what another had said, no student was asked to explain something they understood to a student who didn't understand. The closest he got to that was something like 'Did you hear what Jane just said? You multiply both sides by two.' This was a sorry attempt at having students share ideas with each other!" Maria was also critical of the teacher's questioning: "The only types of questions this teacher asked were 'What do I do next to solve this problem?'." Maria had suggestions for better types of questions: "The class never considered questions like,

Why we are taking this next step? What would happen if we took this different next step instead? How do you know that is the next step to take? What is the question asking us? What should the answer look like—a number, a set of points, an equation?"

Despite the fact that Maria was disappointed in the instructional practice of this teacher, she did recognize the possibility that the teacher knew the subject matter and probably knew his students:

> From what I could tell, the teacher had, in general, a pretty good knowledge about his students—which ones were following, and which ones would most likely be able to follow. He knew that they cared about grades and Regents exam scores (which isn't actually true of every class or every student), and knew which ones were the troublemakers, not doing their work and not trying. He definitely knew the actual mathematics itself, and he knew the Regents curriculum—what the Regents will expect from the students.

Maria attributed what she believed was his inferior teaching style to his lack of knowledge of suitable pedagogy. She said: "I don't believe he understands how the students learn or what is best for their learning."

Based on what she observed, Maria was able to deduce this teacher's beliefs about his role and the students' roles in his classroom: "I think he sees his role as a teacher as solely to get them to do well on the Regents exam by showing them the material and forcing them to do work by means of holding grades over their heads. I think he sees the students as a passive audience that can sometimes contribute to his presentation (but only with right answers—he doesn't like wrong answers), and whose active learning takes place through homework."

Maria's conjecture regarding the teacher's beliefs about mathematics was not a result of her observation of how he represented mathematics to his students. Rather, she expressed her own belief about all mathematics teachers, which may or may not be accurate: "It was not clear from the class I observed that the teacher feels that mathematics is anything special or dynamic, but I must give him the benefit of the doubt and imagine that he does on some level. It is impossible for me to consider that someone would be a math teacher and not have at least some of these beliefs about mathematics." Maria reasoned that this teacher was unable to transfer his appreciation for mathematics to his students because it was not part of his goals: "This teacher's only goal was to cause the students to do well on the Regents by means of learning some math."

Maria recognized the distinction between monitoring as a means of finding out which students were on task and monitoring as a means to learn about what the students understood:

> The teacher definitely monitored the students to see if they were following. He called on almost all of the students throughout the course of the period, many of whom had not had their hands up. However, he never asked how a student got an answer, so he really couldn't know if the student who answered correctly was just guessing, or what mistake the student who answered incorrectly had made. Therefore, his method of monitoring couldn't really give him an accurate assessment of the students' knowledge or thoughts.

Maria's idea that the teacher did not monitor to assess student understanding was reasonable because, as she pointed out, he did not seem to deviate from his planned lesson, despite indications from the students that maybe he should have.

Regarding the category of regulating Maria said, "The teacher refused to adjust his proposed lesson to the needs of the students. When it was clear that a few of the students weren't positive about how to factor the quadratic, he said 'you should know this' and just did it, not explaining how in detail or taking even a minute to explain (or better yet, have another student explain) what was happening."

Maria was disappointed, but not surprised, that this teacher did not have the time to talk to her about the lesson so that she could examine his postactive thoughts. However, from what she has said, we can see that Maria has developed a keen observatory eye and is able to relate the underlying teacher cognitions that are probably at work. This is a giant step on the road to becoming a teacher who can engage in self-assessment and reflection at a deep level of understanding and insight.

Ruth observed a review lesson on the properties of parallelograms. In her report she pointed out many ways that the teacher could have made the lesson more motivating for students and many strategies the teacher could have used to get them actively involved. However, in her interview with the teacher following the lesson, the teacher never addressed any strategies for improving the quality of the lesson.

> After the lesson, I was able to talk with the teacher to see how he felt about the lesson. He told me that this was a review for them but it was a subject he needed to make sure they knew. He had hoped to be able to

start proofs with them today but decided it would be better to start it with them tomorrow. He had planned to give a quiz on Friday and it was going to include what they had done today in class. Since they didn't get to everything he had planned, he was going to either revise the quiz or postpone it for another day.

Ruth reacted to the teacher's assessment of his lesson: "I was glad to see that the teacher is using the information he obtained from the way the class went today in order to revise his plans for tomorrow and the rest of the unit. What confuses me is that since this was such a teacher-centered class and the teacher did almost all of the talking and all of the explaining, I don't know how he even knew the students needed more time on the topic."

Ruth pointed out a critical problem with self-assessment and how this teacher would be unlikely to recognize a need to change: "I guess I would be fooling myself if I ever thought this teacher would come out of this lesson saying he should have gotten more input from the students. He has been teaching this way for many years, and he has been getting a fair amount of students to pass the tests. Why should he think he needs to do things differently?" In a few short sentences, Ruth has placed her finger on why so many teachers, entrenched in their own practice, will probably never change. Hopefully, after being exposed to questions about every aspect of her instructional practice, when she is asked to reflect on her own lessons, Ruth will go far beyond what this teacher thought about.

Chapter 6

Using the Model to Examine Your Own Instructional Practice and Cognitions

The fact that teachers' cognitions are the driving force behind their behaviors in the classroom makes it essential that whenever you analyze your own teaching, you incorporate assessments of your own thoughts and decision making as well as your instructional practices. In this book, the model we present provides the conceptual basis for approaches you, as a preservice teacher, can use to reflect on and assess your teaching in a structured way. As suggested in previous chapters, the lesson plan you write and your instructional practice are only part of your work. The cognitions that you have before you write your lesson plan, the thoughts you have while teaching your lesson, and the thoughts you have after you have completed your lesson are also critical components of teaching. To facilitate analyses of cognitions and instructional practices before, during, and after lessons, we recommend participating in written and verbal pre- and postlesson activities. Although you cannot be expected to write pre- and postlesson activities on a daily basis, writing your plans and thoughts when your supervisor or a peer observes you or for a videotaped lesson can be an excellent tool for professional growth. In addition, if you get accustomed to thinking about your lesson in such a structured manner, it is likely that it will become a natural part of your reflective practice (even though it may not be in written form). It is this application of the model that is explained and exemplified in the remainder of this chapter.

REFLECTION AND SELF-ASSESSMENT
WITH THE ASSISTANCE OF A SUPERVISOR
OR COOPERATING TEACHER

To prepare for a lesson that your supervisor or cooperating teacher will observe, write not only your lesson plan but also a description of your prelesson thoughts and concerns. Presenting these documents before starting the lesson gives your supervisor the background information he or she needs to better understand the lesson. After the lesson, meet with your supervisor to share your impressions and analysis of the lesson, the thoughts you had while teaching the lesson, and your own ideas about how you might do things differently if you were to teach the lesson again. After you have shared your thoughts, the supervisor can share his or her impressions of the lesson and what you have said. At this time, your supervisor can reinforce positive features of the lesson and give suggestions for further thought and improvement. After the conference, think about what you and your supervisor discussed, and submit documents to your supervisor at the next class meeting that include your postlesson thoughts and final assessments. Your supervisor can then use these materials to assess your ability to engage in the reflective and self-assessment skills so necessary for ongoing improvement in teaching. Each of these activities is structured in a way that is consistent with the conceptual model described earlier in this book. The details of these activities follows as well as excerpts from the work of our student teachers. Detailed guides for the written observation reports and the conference are in Appendix D-1.

Prelesson Thoughts: Reflecting on Your Preactive
and Interactive Cognitions Before Teaching a Lesson

There are many reasons why it is important to write your prelesson thoughts and present them to your supervisor before teaching a lesson. First, it is a way to communicate with your supervisor and set the stage for your lesson. This is your opportunity to justify your plans for this lesson and a time to explain the dilemmas and frustrations you may be facing. You want to be sure that when the supervisor sits down to observe your lesson, she or he understands the context for instruction that has contributed to your decision making for that class. The second critical purpose of writing the thoughts you have before or during lesson planning is to make explicit to your supervisor, as well as to yourself, your overarching cognitions. It is important that you write about the goals you have for your students and what you know about them. Becoming student focused helps you to advance more quickly from the initial stage of teaching, where content is the main focus, to the latter stages of teaching, where student understanding is the main focus.

We also suggest that you write about the knowledge you have of the mathematical content and the methods of pedagogy suitable for this lesson. This process encourages you to get a better understanding and appreciation of the content, see a bigger picture of the content, and focus on and consider alternative strategies for conducting the lesson. Including information about the resources you used to create the lesson encourages you to go beyond the textbook when making decisions about how to teach a lesson. Consulting a variety of sources (e.g., other texts, journals especially written for mathematics teachers, other teachers in the school, peers, books, the Internet) increases your knowledge and makes your lessons more interesting and effective.

Finally, although you might write a lesson plan with a detailed script to follow, remember that, as in every human endeavor, things don't always go as planned. As you become more experienced, you will be able to anticipate when problems might arise and what to do when they occur. This is the art of being able to engage in effective on-the-spot monitoring and regulating of classroom instruction. To help prepare you for this challenge, try to anticipate the areas of difficulty you might face as you teach your lesson and create a plan for dealing with these difficulties in case they do arise.

Although beliefs are a key component of the overarching cognitions in the model, it is not directly addressed in your assignment for prelesson thoughts. There is an important and interesting reason for this. By the time you are ready for student teaching, you have a clear idea of the latest philosophies of mathematics instruction that are valued, and if asked about your beliefs regarding mathematics instruction, you know what your instructors want to hear and are probably very adept at saying it. In our research (Artzt & Armour-Thomas, 1998), several student teachers gave wonderful lip service to their beliefs about student-centered instruction yet contradicted those ideas during their instructional practice. In fact, when interviewed as they viewed videotapes of their lessons, these students often contradicted their prelesson beliefs as they tried to justify their actions. Using the idea that "actions speak louder than words," the supervisor should save all discussion of your beliefs until after the lesson is concluded and you are called on to justify your actions. Essentially, deeply held beliefs are indirectly revealed in all that you do as you teach your lessons.

The details of this prelesson activity follow as well as excerpts from the work of our student teachers.

Provide Personal Background Information

Although student teaching is usually cited as the most valuable experience in a teacher preparation program, it can be fraught with difficulties. For example, conflicts sometimes arise between the philosophies of the supervisor, the student teacher, and the cooperating teacher. Dilemmas sometimes exist between the desire to use interesting teaching strategies and the perception that they will take too long and impede the efforts to "cover the content." Sometimes a cooperating teacher is reluctant to relinquish control of the class to an inexperienced student teacher. Student teachers placed in these kinds of difficult positions have to make serious decisions about the nature of their instructional practice. If any of these problems exist, it is important to inform your supervisor by including them in your prelesson thoughts. Here Jenny describes her frustrations after student teaching for eight weeks:

> Before I start writing about my prelesson thoughts, I think I need to write a little bit about the class, my cooperating teacher, and my experience with the class. I have only been in front of the class about five times so far, and only one of these has been to teach. My cooperating teacher is an extremely nice man but unwilling to give me any freedom in the classroom. He says that the ideas I share with him about teaching or certain materials are good, but he would prefer that I do things his way. That is why, in the lesson you are about to observe, you will see that I am just going to explain the material to the kids in a very straightforward way.

Having read what Jenny said, the supervisor was much more understanding than she would have been if she had observed such a teacher-centered lesson without this information. It was encouraging to note that Jenny was dissatisfied with the traditional teacher-centered approach she was asked to take. The question then was how to help Jenny formulate a student-centered approach that would be acceptable to the cooperating teacher.

In Catherine's prelesson thoughts, it is easy to sense her frustration with the dull problems she is about to use for the focus of her instruction:

Before I delve into all the interesting problems I wanted to use in this lesson, let me start by saying that I don't. My cooperating teacher wanted me to do a lesson on all the types of Pythagorean theorem questions that are bound to show up on the Regents exam. Although I would have liked to teach this lesson with some examples from carpentry or bridge building or some other real-life example, I had to take all routine problems from the Regents Review Book. They were very drab.

If the supervisor had not read these prelesson thoughts, she would have been unaware that Catherine had such good ideas for applying the Pythagorean theorem and was not using them because of the wishes of the cooperating teacher.

Write About Your Goals for Students

When you describe the goals you have for your students, take into consideration the development of both procedural skills and conceptual understanding. Even though research suggests that the overriding concern of most beginning teachers is content coverage, the important thing to realize is that content coverage only has value in relation to student understanding and skill development. You should also consider goals for your students that are supplementary but intertwined with performance goals. That is, it is important for students to understand the value of learning a specific aspect of mathematics. It is also essential that students feel capable of learning the material and communicating their understanding to others.

Anna explains her goals for students in the prelesson thoughts she wrote for a lesson on adding and subtracting radicals:

> One of my goals is that students will come to understand that adding and subtracting radicals is just an extension of their prior knowledge, and I am hoping that it will not be very difficult for them to do. Also, I want them to be able to check that the rules for this topic are correct by calculating the values of the expressions. By using the interesting real-life problem I found for this topic, I hope that I can help the students recognize and appreciate the use of math in the real world. They will also be required to use problem-solving techniques and think logically.

Anna's goals go far beyond mere procedural competency. She is concerned that students be able to link their new understanding to their past understanding. Furthermore, by having them "check" the rules, it is clear that Anna wants the students to have confidence in what they are learning. Finally, she explicitly states her concern that they see the value in what they are learning.

Write About What You Know About Your Students

The next section of your prelesson thoughts should contain a description of your students and what you know about their ability levels, personalities, and interests. In addition, you should describe the gender, language, and racial/ethnic backgrounds of your students. In the beginning of a semester, your accounts might be general in nature, but as the semester progresses, you should be able to be quite detailed in your descriptions. For example, it is not enough to say that students have difficulty learning different counting procedures. This is too vague a comment to provide a focus for the design of the lesson. Rather, you should outline the specific difficulties that the students are having. That is, it is more helpful to say that students have difficulty deciding when to use combinations and when to use permutations. Such comments will help you to design a lesson that focuses on and highlights clearly the difference between the two counting procedures.

Margaret identifies a specific area of difficulty for her students:

I feel that students need more time and practice with permutations, even though they've learned it in the past. Yesterday, while circulating, I realized that some students did not understand why $15!/14! = 15$. I saw that some students in class grasp probability ideas quickly where others didn't know what we were doing. As time progresses, I learn more about each student. Now I think I know who to pair up so that the ones who understand it can help the ones who don't.

Not only is Margaret specific in her evaluations of what her students understand, but she has come to know their abilities and is now in a position to use that knowledge to their advantage in the classroom.

Nora chooses to focus on the students' self-confidence and disposition toward mathematics when revealing her knowledge of students:

To get them interested in quadrilaterals and make the concepts easier to understand, for homework I asked them to cut out strips of given lengths from cardboard I distributed. Some of the students commented, "I could not even pass algebra. How can I pass geometry?" It is really challenging to motivate some of the students in this class because they are so disappointed with their abilities that they don't even try to understand.

It is clear that Nora is trying to adapt her teaching to the knowledge she has of her students' low self-esteem in mathematics.

An excerpt from Karen's prelesson thoughts shows that she is considering the ability levels and language differences that exist in her class:

> There is a wide range of ability levels in the class, so I will have to think of the brightest student as well as the slowest. I am concerned about some of the students who have language problems though. I am beginning to plan a lesson where they will have to describe various shapes. Although this will be difficult for them, I believe it may serve as a good practice.

Although Karen is not explicit about how she intends to meet the needs of the wide range of student ability in the class, it is good that she is aware that they exist and that her intention is to meet all of their needs.

Vanessa's prelesson thoughts shows how her knowledge of students has been progressing over the course of the semester:

> I don't believe I have a firm grasp of my knowledge of students yet. My class seems average; I have some stronger students and some weaker. I also seem to have at least one student who absolutely panics when she sees a math example. In past lessons I've been surprised by what the students did not understand. I'm getting more used to the fact that what may seem simple to me could be far from easy for my students.

Vanessa's last comment indicates that she has arrived at one of the most important realizations a teacher can have. All too often, teachers are unable to put themselves in the place of the learner and recognize what may be problematic for them.

Finally, excerpts from Jasmine's first and fourth observations show how she has learned to deal with a student, Roxanne, because she got to know her better. In her first observation, Jasmine describes how she plans to use a small-group activity but has concerns about Roxanne:

> Since the children are not used to this type of activity, I worry that it can go totally wrong. I also have concerns about one student in particular. Her name is Roxanne, and other teachers have told me to watch out for

her. She can totally change the course of a lesson. She tends to make wisecracks to me during class that are very disruptive. I'm not sure what her problem is.

By the fourth observation, Jasmine has taken the time to get to know Roxanne, whose behavior has completely changed:

I have met many times with Roxanne after class and have spoken to her personally about why she makes the comments she does. Even though she couldn't give me any reason, I think she just needed that personal attention. I am embarrassed to say I had a preconceived opinion of Roxanne because of other people's opinion of her. I am very happy to say Roxanne has become one of my most treasured students in the class. Roxanne often does change the course of my lesson, but I wish I had a dollar for each thoughtful, wonderful question she asks during our lessons. When introducing parabolas, Roxanne was the one to ask, "What happens if we turn it upside down?" I could not ask for a better way to introduce $y = -x^2$. I truthfully hope Roxanne learned as much from me as I learned from her this semester.

Jasmine has learned the importance of taking the time to really get to know your students so that you can better meet their needs, and in turn, they can better meet your needs.

Write About What You Know About the Content of the Lesson

The next section of your prelesson thoughts should be a written account of what you know about the content. Each day's lesson does not occur in a vacuum. It is part of a story that unfolds throughout the course of the semester, so it is essential that you consider the whole picture when designing the lesson plan. In your prelesson thoughts, describe the mathematical content that came before and the content that will come after that particular day's lesson. Furthermore, describe the value of the content for students. Considering such issues about the content will help you to design a lesson that is sequenced appropriately and will attract the interest of the students.

Yali describes her knowledge of the content, how it relates to what the students learned before and will learn in the future, and the importance of the topic:

We have already studied matrix operations, such as addition, subtraction, scalar multiplication, and matrix multiplication. Also, we have evaluated the determinant of a 2×2 matrix. Today they will learn determinants of a 3×3 matrix by seeing that they must use what they know already (make the 3×3 into a 2×2). Later in the week, they will use the determinant in Cramer's Rule and solving equations. They will then be able to apply these concepts to linear programming which has so many important applications in real life.

Yali's knowledge of matrices has contributed to her ability to sequence the instruction in such a way that her students can build on their previous understanding of 2×2 matrices to learn about 3×3 matrices.

Michele demonstrates her overall knowledge of the content of counting principles and their use in probabilities:

Students have reviewed simple probability, the counting principle, probabilities with two or more activities, as well as permutations. Students were also introduced to permutations with repetitions but did not study probabilities that involve permutations. During this lesson students will be introduced to a new concept—combinations. During the next several days, they will practice problems and find probabilities using either permutations or combinations, so they must learn to distinguish when to use which.

It is clear that Michele understands that students learn the counting principles to solve problems in probability and that it is important for students to understand the distinctions between permutations and combinations. This broad picture is often what eludes students and makes topics confusing for them. Michele's depth of understanding is likely to facilitate her ability to help her students understand the concepts.

Write About What You Know About Pedagogical Approaches for the Lesson

When you write about your knowledge of different pedagogical approaches that might be suitable for your lesson, include descriptions of the roles that you and the students will play in the lesson. This will help you to decide which approach might work best. You should also consider which tools and motivational techniques will be most suitable for helping students to gain conceptual understanding. This task is designed to help you envision the engagement and interaction between you and the students during the lesson. It is also designed to help you consider different options for the representations that will work best in helping students to understand the concepts.

The following two excerpts from the prelesson thoughts of Julie and Eileen illustrate a focus on materials that would be most effective for their particular lessons. Julie writes:

> Since my goal is to reintroduce area, I would like to build a lesson out of what they may already know about the topic. I would like to use something physical, where they can visually see that the area of a triangle is half of a rectangle with the same base and height. I would have liked to use geoboards; however, there are a few students who I would not trust working with rubber bands. I may use graph paper as a substitute for the geoboard, or use tangrams to explore area with problem solving.

Regardless of whether Julie has made a good decision to forego using geoboards, the important point is that she has used her knowledge of students to impact her choice for instruction.

Eileen weighs the pros and cons of using different materials to use for a lesson on the graphing of parabolas:

> A graphing calculator can be used in this lesson so not as much time will be spent on graphing parabolas. On the other hand, students need practice in graphing, and perhaps it would be a little confusing to students to see that on a calculator the parabola does not look really as a smooth curve, and the units on the x-axis and y-axis on a calculator are usually not the same, so that the parabola drawn on graph paper and the one on the calculator may look a little different. Also, I am not super familiar with a graphing calculator, so I will choose to use colored markers and an overhead projector.

Eileen's inadequate knowledge of the graphing calculator has influenced her choice of materials. However, she is able to come up with alternative approaches.

Latisha's prelesson thoughts reveal that her pedagogical concerns center around the mode of instruction she will use to discuss the fairness of a particular game of dice. Although Latisha is convinced that the game has to be enacted, she debates in her mind how to do it:

I would have liked to have split the class into groups of three and have each group do the experiment so that we would have lots of trials and so that the students could work together and be more actively involved. However, I will not do it that way because my cooperating teacher said it would be difficult to get that many pairs of dice. So I will choose three students to do the experiment in the front of the room while the rest of the class watches.

Clearly, Latisha appreciates the value of getting all students actively involved in the lesson.

Finally, Katie's prelesson thoughts show that she is well aware of a variety of pedagogical strategies:

In this lesson, I will use three types of instructional formats: small-group discussion, group presentation, and whole-class discussion. I am using these formats in the hopes that within the small groups, the students will get a chance to share ideas with their peers; within the group presentation, the students will get the opportunity to share their findings with the entire class; within the large class discussion, the students will get an opportunity to develop an understanding of algebraic expressions through hearing each others' questions and comments.

Katie indicates that she knows not only a variety of teaching strategies but also the specific advantages each has for student learning.

Write About the Sources You Will Consult for Designing the Lesson

In this section of your prelesson thoughts, describe the sources you used to get ideas for the lesson and the criteria you used for making your final selections. When designing a lesson, it is a good idea to use many different sources of information. Doing so encourages you to use different resources as a means for increasing your knowledge and expanding your alternatives with respect to the design of the lesson. There is no reason to "reinvent the wheel" when designing a lesson.

Every school usually has a mathematics office with a small library. You might consult different textbooks for ideas. There is a wealth of interesting material published by the National Council of Teachers of Mathematics (NCTM). In addition, there are many materials created as a result of government and private funding. In addition, you can find interesting ideas for lessons on the Internet. However, remember that as of now, there is no quality control on the Internet, and some of these materials have not been edited. It is also important to consult with experienced teachers in your school who probably have a wealth of ideas just waiting to be shared.

Greg's prelesson thoughts clearly show that he has learned the value of consulting with other people as a source for good ideas: "The idea for this lesson (finding Waldo) came from Anna, a fellow student teacher, who in turn got it from her cooperating teacher, Etta. It worked well in their classes, so it seemed like it was worth a chance here."

In her prelesson thoughts, Angelina chooses to describe the process she used in working with a variety of sources:

> The materials used for this lesson plan are: Sequential Mathematics Course II Part 2 lesson plans written by the NYC Board of Education; Barron's Review Course on Sequential Math; and the textbook. I first viewed the textbook to see how the topic was discussed. I then compared it to the Lesson Plan book. Then I would pick and choose depending on how it was presented. Class problems were picked from the Barron's Review Book and the Lesson Plan book, thus reducing the chance of giving a problem that was done in class for homework. Though I wonder if they look at their notes. Homework assignments have basically come out of the textbook.

Irina's prelesson thoughts demonstrate that she has learned to use different sources—other teachers as well as written sources—in combination: "I got this idea from the eighth grade curriculum book that the district wrote. This is the first year they have implemented the new curriculum. I also researched ideas from the *Mathematics Teacher,* as well as conferring with my cooperating teacher and other teachers." Most schools have teachers who are eager to mentor novice teachers. Unfortunately, many beginning teachers are too shy or embarrassed to take advantage of their expertise and generosity. It is good to see that Irina has availed herself of this wonderful resource.

Write About Difficulties You Anticipate and How You Intend to Prepare for Them

No matter how carefully you have planned your lesson, the likelihood is that things will not proceed exactly as planned. It is important that you develop the ability to sense when a change is needed and what the appropriate change should be. That is, you need to develop your ability to monitor the lesson and regulate your instruction accordingly. The trick to dealing with unexpected events is to anticipate what they will be and plan what to do should they occur. The more experience you get, the easier it will be for you to predict problems you might encounter and the appropriate adjustments to make. For example, you will come to know what concepts students tend get hung up on and the examples you can give to clarify the confusion. You will learn good approximations for the length of time different pedagogical strategies will take. You will also learn how to predict certain students' behaviors and plan appropriate roles and activities for these students. Even though you are a novice teacher, it is not too early to begin to anticipate difficulties that may occur in your lesson and make appropriate plans.

In the excerpt from Sarah's prelesson thoughts, she demonstrates her awareness of the different attention spans and knowledge of her students and how that may impact her plans for her lesson on developing a formula for permutations with repetition:

> The problem I am anticipating is that it takes awhile to generate each sample space and I think some of them lose interest, particularly those that fully understand and are bored. Also, a few of them may know the mystery formula, having learned it on their own. I hope they don't spill the beans. If someone does this, I'm going to insist that they justify why the formula works. It is not enough to just plug in the formula.

Although she does not express a plan for what to do if the students do "lose interest," Sarah does have a plan in case a student gives the formula away before the students develop it on their own.

Tara expresses two areas of concern in her prelesson thoughts:

> A main concern is avoiding arithmetic error. I always second-guess myself. I rush to get the answer, and I make mistakes and look like an idiot. I've tried to familiarize myself with the examples, and I've written the answers down to avoid humiliation. My biggest concern is timing. The few times I've taught lessons, I've either run out of time or there's too much time. I can honestly say I have no idea how long it will take to finish each section. My cooperating teacher always says, "They're very bright, and you can move quickly." But sometimes I'm shocked at what it is they have a problem with.

Although Tara has a detailed plan for how to combat her problem with making arithmetic errors when in front of the class, she is still perplexed by the issue of timing. However, it is good to see that her concerns about timing involve her concerns that students understand the material.

Fran expresses concerns about behavioral problems when students work in groups: "Since I have had some behavioral problems in this class when they work in groups, I am expecting some problems. However, this task is very specific, unlike other group work I have had them engaged in." It is reassuring to note that rather than giving up on using small-group work for these students, Fran has instead planned a way to make it work better.

Finally, Ellie, who was teaching the family unit from the Interactive Mathematics Program, shows an awareness of the difficulty students may have with a particular lesson:

> I believe that the most challenging part of this lesson will be getting started on the families. Some students may become bogged down by the usage of *at most, at least,* etc. As such, I plan on walking around while they are working in their groups and helping elicit a better understanding of these terms. In addition I will call the class to attention and have some of the students explain their understanding of these terms and how they use this understanding to construct their families.

It is reassuring to note that Ellie intends to monitor the understanding of her students. Although she has not stated how she will resolve confusion about the words, she has prepared herself for where the trouble may arise.

Summary

By giving descriptions of your prelesson thoughts, not only are you encouraged to think about the overarching cognitions that drive your lesson, but it gives your supervisor, who subsequently observes the lesson, insight into the decision making and reasoning behind your lesson. Knowing why you do what you do when you are teaching makes it easier for your supervisor to understand and assess the instruction he or she observes. Directions for writing your prelesson thoughts are in Appendix D-2.

Creating a Lesson Plan Consistent with Your Cognitions

The prelesson thoughts that you have written should serve as the foundation for the creation of your lesson plan. Starting with the objectives for student performance and understanding set forth by the NCTM (1989, 2000), you can set goals that go far beyond mere performance objectives. You want students to value mathematics, have confidence in their ability to do mathematics, and engage in such mathematical processes as problem solving, reasoning and proof, communication, and making connections and representations.

You can derive the structure of your lesson from your knowledge of the students, the content, and pedagogical strategy. The sequencing of the tasks must come from your knowledge of the logical sequencing of the content and students' prior understandings. The motivation for the lesson may be developed through the creation of a void in the students' knowledge, in which case you need a clear awareness of students' level of understanding. Motivation may also be created by linking to something in real life that is of interest to your students. Such a motivational strategy can only be effective if you are well informed about the interests and backgrounds of each student. Different content areas lend themselves to different motivational strategies. Therefore, a thorough understanding of the nature of the content is needed to design appropriate motivational approaches. Finally, you can derive effective instructional strategies from your knowledge of the content, the students, and pedagogy. For example, the discovery approach only lends itself to content that is within reach of student ability and can be derived from students' previous knowledge. You must have a good grasp of the content and the ability levels of your students to use this approach effectively. Furthermore, you must be aware of how different instructional strategies can facilitate or impede student discovery. For example, in many cases, a small-group approach, in which each student in the group works on a similar activity to derive a pattern and generalization, is the most effective way of facilitating discovery learning. You need to be well versed in small-group strategies to enable such an approach.

The phases of the lesson also grow out of a teacher's underlying cognitions. That is, the *initiation* of a lesson requires that you establish your students' readiness for learning the new content. This necessitates that you have a good understanding of the content and the prerequisite knowledge that is needed to learn the new content. The *development* of a lesson requires the building of new understandings. In the creation of the plan, you must employ all that you know about different pedagogical approaches, the structure of the mathematical concepts, and the distinct abilities and interests of the students to design an effective development.

The *closure* phase of the lesson is the time when the new concepts are integrated with the students' previous understandings and, when possible, extensions of the concepts are made. Creating culminating activities that promote the integration and extension of concepts demands a depth of understanding of the concept that goes beyond the mere requirements of the curriculum.

This chapter does not include examples of lesson plans because this aspect of your instruction should be well covered in the methods textbook you are using in conjunction with this book. However, Appendix D-2 includes an outline for writing a lesson plan.

Reflecting on Your Instructional Practice During the Lesson: Monitoring and Regulating

Effective monitoring and regulating is a part of teaching that is often described as the art of teaching. It consists of the thousands of moment-to-moment decisions that teachers make during the course of their lessons based on the feedback they receive as they enact the lessons. Often these decisions take the lessons down paths that the teachers did not plan. Being able to diverge from the original lesson plan to better meet the needs of students is the mark of quality teaching. Often beginning teachers are distressed when they do not accomplish all their plans for their lessons. They need to view this in a more positive light, understanding that teaching is much like problem solving. That is, you may set out with a specific plan, but if things are not proceeding the way you wish, you must have the flexibility to make some alterations. Also, as in problem solving, it is essential to monitor the progress of the lesson. This entails engaging students in a way that allows them to tell you, through their remarks and behaviors, whether they are indeed learning. You must then have the willingness and ability to change the course of your lesson if necessary.

Your postlesson conference is a good time for you to reflect on and assess the monitoring and regulating you engaged in during the course of your lesson.

Reflecting on Your Instructional Practice After the Lesson: Evaluating and Revising

After you have completed your lesson, set aside time to meet with your supervisor to reflect on and assess your instructional practice and your thoughts related to that practice. Keep in mind that it is important that you express your ideas before anybody else gives you input regarding their reactions to your lesson. This is the first step in your becoming an independent learner of teaching. Through most of your career, you alone will be in the class with your students, and you will have to reflect on and assess your instruction on your own. Your ability to engage in such self-analysis will determine your professional growth as a teacher. Therefore, it is important for you to develop the habit of being the first critic of your own teaching. We have found that student teachers often have a difficult time analyzing their lessons. They tend to make such general comments as "I think it went OK," or "That was a disaster." Some students just draw a blank and can't even remember what happened. That is why we provide a detailed structure that, through appropriate questions, allows you to analyze every aspect of your instructional practice as well as your cognitions. This structure is explained in the following sections.

Express Your Thoughts About the Lesson to the Supervisor

With the help of the written guide given in Appendix D-1, assess your own lesson while the supervisor and cooperating teacher sit quietly and listen to what you are saying. First, examine how your prelesson thoughts, your lesson plans, and your lesson enactments are related. For example, recall your original goals for the lesson, how you addressed them in the lesson plan, and to what extent you believe you accomplished your goals. You should compare what you planned to do in the lesson with what you actually did. Explain how you decided to deviate or not to deviate from your original plans. That is, you should explain your monitoring and regulating behaviors as you taught the lesson. For example, you might describe what feedback you received from the students and how it informed your practice.

Following this discussion, in case all aspects of the lesson have not been addressed, further assess your lesson with a focus on the elements: tasks, learning environment, and discourse. Think about, describe, and evaluate the nature of these elements as they unfolded in your classroom. Consider reasons that might have contributed to the nature of your lesson. Finally, consider suggestions you might have for improving your lesson if you were to teach it again.

The Supervisor Shares His or Her Thoughts About the Lesson and the Thoughts You Have Expressed

After you have completed your own postlesson reflection and assessment, your supervisor and cooperating teacher should share their thoughts regarding the lesson. The supervisor can provide positive reinforcement when appropriate and request clarification of issues by using the model as a basis for helping you to think about and appreciate what new knowledge you have gained or beliefs you may have changed as a result of teaching the lesson. Your supervisor might ask such questions as: What have you learned as a result of teaching this lesson? What have you learned about the content, the students, or the best ways of teaching the lesson? What beliefs did you have about the content, the students, or the best ways of teaching the lesson that changed in some way?

It is important for you and the supervisor to remember that the focus of this conference is not to judge how good or bad the lesson was. Teaching is a learning process, and we hope you are in it for the long haul. Therefore, the primary goal of the conference is for you to learn more about yourself and your teaching so that you will continue to improve. In our program, we base student grades not on our judgment of the quality of the lessons they teach but rather on what we believe they have learned from the process of learning how to teach. We are most interested in how student teachers reflect on and assess their lessons *after* having conferences with their supervisors. That is the purpose of the written postlesson, postconference activity.

Write Your Postlesson, Postconference Reflections, and Assessment

After the conference with your supervisor, put your thoughts about the lesson in writing. Written documentation of your thoughts and assessment serves at least two purposes. First, it gives you the opportunity to reflect on and assess the lesson once again and integrate and synthesize your ideas and those of your supervisor regarding the lesson. Second, it gives the supervisor the opportunity to assess what you have learned from your experience and how you have internalized the ideas that you discussed. With this assessment, she or he can help you improve. Appendix D-3 provides a guide to writing your postlesson thoughts and assessment.

To help you assess the nature and quality of the dimensions of your lesson, first complete the Self-Assessment of Instructional Practice form that appears in Appendix D-4. This form asks you to rate and describe each dimension of your instructional practice. For example, according to Table 1, which lists the lesson dimensions and dimension indicators, the indicator for a quality motivational strategy for the tasks dimension is, "Uses tasks that capture students' curiosity and inspires them to speculate and to pursue their conjectures. The diversity of student interests and experiences must be taken into account. The substance of the motivation is aligned with the goals and purposes of instruction." Based on that description, you can rate the motivational strategy used in your lesson. A rating of 3 represents a strong presence of the indicator, a 2 represents the indicator is somewhat present, and a 1 indicates that there is no presence of the indicator. In addition to rating the dimension, the form requires you to make a short comment. For example, a student who rated her motivation as a 3 made the following comment: "The guessing game was motivational because it caught the students' attention."

The guide in Appendix D-3 asks you to revisit some of the questions you addressed during your conference, reflecting on the degree to which you accomplished your original goals for the lesson. You describe how your knowledge or beliefs were changed in any way as a result of the teaching experience and the conference. You also describe the thoughts you had and the basis of your decisions while teaching the lesson. An important question you are asked to consider is how well you think you evaluated your own lesson prior to hearing the ideas of your supervisor or cooperating teacher. Finally, you highlight the strong points and areas of the lesson that need improvement and the cognitions that might have been the contributing factors to these aspects of your lessons. Include suggestions of ways to improve the lesson, and submit a revised lesson plan if your suggestions are extensive.

To show how some of our student teachers have integrated their understanding of the relationship between their cognitions and their instructional practices, the following sections give sample responses to the questions that appear in Appendix D-3.

Goals.   Consider your original goals for the lesson. Did you accomplish these goals? How do you know?

In Marissa's response to the question regarding goal accomplishment, she distinguishes between students' understanding of the concepts and their ability to carry out the procedure. Her perception is that the students did not arrive at a conceptual understanding of the content:

> I did not accomplish the goal that I had to have the students understand the use of the property of zero and factoring to solve quadratic equations. I know this because at the end of my lesson I asked the class, "Why did the quadratic equations have to be equal to zero before we could solve them?" They had no idea. One boy read the rule about ab=0, but he didn't know how it was connected to the factoring and the equation.

However, she recognizes that surprisingly, despite their lack of conceptual understanding, the students were able to solve the problems: "I did accomplish the goal that was to have the students learn the procedure for solving a quadratic equation. I know this because at the end of the lesson, I went around to see how they were doing with the last three questions, and they were solving the equations."

Marissa wisely used student feedback as the source for her assessment of whether or not her goals were accomplished.

Knowledge.   Describe what new ideas you may have learned about the content, the students, or the best ways of teaching the lesson.

In her postlesson comments, Janine indicates that she learned much about ways of improving dimensions of her instructional practice. She indicates her increased knowledge of how to conduct discourse when she says, "I learned that when students are very quiet, say less and let them say more." Her change in knowledge about what constitutes motivation is evident in her comment, "I learned that an 'attention catcher' is not necessarily motivation. Motivation is the question that comes from the attention catcher. The motivational question should be stressed." Janine also indicates her increased knowledge about how to teach concepts:

> I learned that before I present a general concept to the class, I should give several specific cases first as well as some non-examples. In this lesson, I presented only one case of parallel lines. I should have given three or four examples of parallel lines and at least one case where the lines were not parallel. This way the students could have discovered the pattern of the slopes when two lines are parallel.

Beliefs.   Describe what beliefs you had about the content, the students, or the best ways of teaching the lesson that changed in some way.

Leah's comments reveal a change in her beliefs about her role as a teacher: "The students were very responsive and asked many interesting and important questions. Unfortunately, I felt obligated to answer every question. I should try to throw the questions back to the class. I tend to listen to what the student is asking, but then I answer the question myself instead of involving the class." It appears that Leah is beginning to reconsider her belief that her role is to be the "answer-person" for the students.

Following her lesson, Lauren found she had new beliefs about students' knowledge:

> I also believed that my students remembered what they had learned before about solving linear systems of equations. Unfortunately, many students forgot what a system of equations was. From this experience, I learned that we should never assume that students remember past lessons. We should poke their memories by spiraling homework that pertains to the upcoming lesson.

Lauren has not only changed her beliefs about how much students retain from past lessons, but she has a plan for how to cope with the problem.

After her lesson, Sonya was questioning her beliefs about students:

> I previously believed that students (particularly seniors) understood that when I begin looking at and talking to the whole class and a problem is being solved on the board, they are to listen. Apparently, you have to spell that out, as after the Do Now was put up and there was a discussion going on, a group of boys on the side were not with us because I didn't specifically tell them to be!

Monitoring and Regulating.   What were some of the thoughts you had during the lesson that caused you to make the decisions you made? Beryl mentions two very different instances of monitoring and regulating during the course of her lesson. In the first instance, she monitored student involvement and made a decision she felt worked out well:

> One thought that I had during the lesson was, "Wow, the students are really tired and out of it." I knew that I had to do something about this. I decided to ask students to go up to the board to solve problems while the rest worked at their desks. As they worked, I walked around and asked

the tired students, "Are you O.K.?" After asking this, these students woke up and participated.

In the second instance, she monitored the work that was on the board and made a decision she felt worked out terribly:

> While going over the homework, I noticed that one of the assigned problems was not on the board. At first I thought that the best way to handle this situation was to forget about the problem. However, I saw that many students had problems with this question. Thus, I decided to ask a student to go to the board and do the problem. This decision, however, was not wise. While the student was writing her answer on the board, the other students sat idle. I will never do this again.

The important point about Beryl's comments is that she reveals her sensitivity to what is going on in her class and her willingness to make on-the-spot adjustments.

Nora also reveals her insight into on-the-spot decision making during her class. She mentions two interesting situations. In the first instance she describes how monitoring and regulating served to clarify a concept: "I am getting better at monitoring the understanding of the students, such as when Melanie drew a perpendicular in the triangles and everyone became confused. I saw the confusion and was able to clear it up by tracing the two triangles with colored chalk." In the second instance, Nora describes how she monitored a situation, but her lack of regulating contributed to the failure of the lesson:

> On the other hand, although I knew the class was not proceeding as expected, I was aware the task was taking too long, but I did not make the cognitive connection to change the task from one of discovery to one of modeling. Because of that, we ran out of time and I don't think the students learned very much . . .. I believe this will come with time, as every time I sit down to write a lesson plan I am able to anticipate more and more places where trouble may arise and how to compensate for it. This should have been something I anticipated and now experiencing it, it will be something I will be more prepared for in the future.

Nora herself has recognized that becoming an effective on-the-spot decision maker is critical to good teaching, and that experience is gradually helping her to become better at it.

Evaluating and Suggesting.   How well do you feel you evaluated the lesson at the postlesson conference? What points are you aware of now that you weren't aware of then, if any?

Carla's postlesson comments reveal that after teaching the lesson, she only had a general impression of the quality of the lesson and was not able to identify the specifics:

> I believe my overall impression of the lesson was correct at the postles-son conference, that being it was a disaster. Yet, at the time I was not aware of all the reasons why. I see now that the problem was never posed correctly, that the mode of representation was not followed through as planned, that the lesson plan had major gaps in it, that I did a poor job of monitoring and regulating, and that I could never plan to summarize a lesson with goals that were never really set.

Carla taught this lesson at the beginning of the semester. It is interesting to note how she improved in her ability to critique her lessons over the course of the semester. This is what she has to say about the postlesson analysis she gave for a lesson she taught at the end of the semester:

> Now that I can think straight after my lesson is over, I notice that I always tend to vent the worst things at the postlesson conference. Again, because the mode of representation was not the most appropriate one, I believed the goals of the lesson were not accomplished. I no longer believe this to be the case. The students did do the required construc-tions, even though we did not get to the further explorations....I believe I tend to deemphasize some of my most important attributes, such as my rapport with the students. The classroom is a friendly environment where the students feel free to express themselves.

It is interesting to note that by the end of the semester, Carla became so self-critical that she tended not to acknowledge the positive aspects of her lessons.

Since the point of this book is to help you see the relationship of cog-nitions and instructional practice, the questions in this section that ask you to assess the strengths and weaknesses of your lesson do not include examples because they focus mainly on the nature of the instructional practice and are quite standard in teacher education programs. These questions require you to identify the strong points of the lesson, the parts of the lesson that need improvement, and ways to improve the lesson. The self-assessment form for summarizing these aspects of your instructional practice is in Appendix D-5.

Supervisor Evaluates Your Reflections and Assessments

In addition to your self-assessment, your supervisor evaluates your ability to reflect on and assess your instructional practice. At this point, your supervisor has observed you teaching a lesson, has conferenced with you, and is in possession of some critical documents: your prelesson thoughts, your lesson plan, your ratings and summary statements of your assessment of your instructional practice, and your written postlesson thoughts and assessment. Your supervisor has already shared his or her thoughts about your instructional practice and is now in a position to focus on your ability to be a reflective, insightful, self-critical mathematics teacher. In addition to making comments on the written documents you have submitted, your supervisor evaluates your cognitions, using the form found in Appendix D-6. Beginning with preactive indicators, your supervisor evaluates the quality of the goals you have for your students and your knowledge of your pupils, the mathematical content, and pedagogical strategies appropriate for teaching the lesson. Using the categories set forth in the model, your supervisor evaluates your lesson plan. An important aspect of the evaluation is your ability to reflect on and assess your lesson when you just finish it, before you have received any input from others. The hope is that by the end of the semester, your self-analytic comments following the lesson will be so detailed, extensive, and on-target, that the supervisor will have little to add. Finally, the supervisor evaluates your ability to understand and assimilate the ideas shared at the conference as well as your ability to give insightful suggestions for improving your lesson. Your ability to excel in all these areas indicates that you will continue to improve on your own throughout your career as a mathematics teacher.

So far in this chapter, we have outlined how the different elements of the model are put into play when a supervisor observes a student teacher. However, we have examined each element in isolation. In the following section, we will show how Kim put all the elements together in her lesson, which her supervisor observed.

An Example of Using All Elements of the Model
Together in a Supervised Lesson

Kim taught a first lesson on plotting a sine curve on a coordinate grid. Her prelesson thoughts, lesson plan, postlesson thoughts, and revised lesson plan reveal that Kim learned a great deal from the experience.

Prelesson Thoughts

Kim's prelesson thoughts indicate that she values both procedural as well as conceptual understanding of the sine curve graphing:

> My goals for this lesson are that students be able to graph a sine curve and understand its connection with the unit circle. I will start with the unit circle drawn on the board and ask the students to fill in the coordinates at 0, 90, 180, 270, & 360 degrees. Then I want to have them make the connection between degrees and radian measures. They know how to convert from one to another, but I do not think they have really made the connection yet. From the unit circle, I will have them plot the points on a graph emphasizing the connection between the graph and unit circle. This will take a new concept (the sine curve) and cognitively connect it to familiar knowledge (unit circle). I could just graph the curve using the graphing calculator, but I think having them plot the points first will help them understand where it is coming from.

> I also want students to think about the change of behavior the curve will have if we increase amplitude and frequency coefficients. They do not know this yet. I could have them graph the curves on the graphing calculator and come up with a conclusion, but instead I want them to conjecture as to what effect these coefficients will have on the curve. Then we can confirm our hypothesis with the use of the calculator.

The way she plans to structure the lesson by linking students' prior knowledge about the unit circle to the graphing of the function indicates both her knowledge of the content and the importance of sequencing as an effective pedagogical strategy. Her decision to use the calculator as a means for reaffirming hypotheses shows her thoughtful approach to motivation as a critical pedagogical issue.

Kim reveals her knowledge about level of difficulty of the different concepts in her lesson when she explains a problem that she foresees: "I do not anticipate much difficulty with the amplitude. I do, however, anticipate some confusion with the curves involving frequency changes, as this is a harder concept for them to grasp." Unfortunately, Kim did not plan a solution in case the problem came up—and it did. She also anticipated that she might be overambitious in her plans for the lesson: "The lesson is set up for one period, although if we have trouble developing the sine curve, we may not get as far as anticipated. I expect this may happen because other teachers have taken one full lesson to develop the sine curve and then another to introduce amplitude and frequency." As it turned out, Kim was quite rigid about covering so much content. This eventually led to the downfall of her lesson.

Finally, in her prelesson thoughts, Kim describes where she got her ideas for the lesson. "The source for today's lesson was taken from a resident teacher, other than my cooperating teacher, and has been modified to accommodate the needs of this class. I find the teachers in this school are a wealth of information and are usually happy to share it." It was good to see that Kim understood the value of consulting experienced teachers for ideas.

Lesson Plan

Topic.
Sine curve

Aim.
How do frequency and amplitude affect the sine curve?

Objectives.
Students will understand how to plot the sine curve.
Students will understand the relationship between the sine curve and the unit circle.
Students will see how the amplitude and frequency affect the sine curve.

Motivation: Create a Void.
Ask students to plot points and graph $y = \sin x$.
Using a handout sheet (with the clear overhead copy), students will learn how to plot the sine curve using coordinates and radian measures obtained from the unit circle.
Working off the unit circle, have students determine and plot the sine coordinate for theta = 0, 90, 180, 270, 360 degrees.

Exploration.

Q: What do you think the curve of 2sin$x$ will look like?

Q: What might change?

Q: How, increase, decrease...? Does it affect the period of the function?

Call on students to graph it on the overhead.

Graph with the graphing calculator on the overhead while students work on calculators.

Q: Does our graph 2sin$x$ agree with the graph on the calculator?

Continue exploration with other sine curves.

Have students describe verbally the change in behavior of the curves.

Further Exploration.

Q: How do you think the graph of sin2x will vary from sin$x$?

Q: What will it look like?

Have a student draw it on the overhead.

Q: Does this change the period of the function? Why or why not?

Continue exploration by graphing other curves.

Compare results on the graphing calculator.

Describe verbally the change in the behavior of the curves.

Practice.

Write the equation of the curve on the handout.

Have students think and then let one write equation on the overhead.

Ask students if this is correct and why or why not?

Summary.

Ask students to write about what they learned about the amplitude and frequency of a trigonometric function.

Postlesson Thoughts

Contrary to the student-centered focus of the prelesson thoughts, the discourse that took place during the lesson was predominantly teacher centered and impeded the effectiveness of this lesson. Kim rushed through the development, doing most of the explaining herself and accepting student answers without explanations. Despite the students' confusion with the graphing of the sine curve, Kim rushed through the examination of amplitude and frequency and was perplexed by the students' lack of interest. In her postlesson conference, Kim was aware that she tried to do too much in one class period, but she was not aware of how her style of discourse prevented her from monitoring the understanding of the students and adapting her lesson to fit their needs. Kim's written postlesson thoughts indicate that she learned a great deal about the importance of monitoring and regulating during a lesson.

Goals.   Kim realizes that she did not meet the goals she had established for this lesson:

> At the conference, I said yes and no when asked if I accomplished my goals. At the time of the conference I believed I had accomplished some of the goals of the lesson, but on reflection, I do not believe this to be so. For if I had accomplished the students' understanding of the sin curve and how to plot it, then they would have been able to apply this knowledge to plot $y = 2\sin x$, and they could not. I believe, as you stated in the conference, that this is due to incomplete development of the lesson.

Believing now that she did not accomplish her goals, Kim suggests a good idea for improvement.

> To improve this, I would use a Do Now, having students fill in the unit circle with coordinates, degree, and radian measures. I would have one student do it on an overhead sheet so they could put it up for the class to see and compare. After I was sure everyone had this in their notes, we could proceed to create a table of values using the unit circle. I think I would stress more the relationship between the radian measure being the x value on the curve and the y coordinate being the y value of the curve. A chart on the board would have helped to clarify this.

Kim goes on to describe another unfulfilled goal and an appropriate suggestion for improvement: "Another goal was to have them explore how the amplitude and frequency affected the sin curve, but before trying to accomplish this, I should have done a more complete job of defining these terms. I could have accomplished this better had I had the students write the definitions on the board and in their notes after they arrived at them."

Knowledge and Beliefs.   In her discussion regarding knowledge and beliefs, Kim shows that she has learned that students can become enthusiastic about a subject only if they understand the subject:

> I have learned from this experience that we can't rush into things just because we want to teach them. If the students are not ready to receive

this information, no matter how hard I try, they will lose interest because they are unsure of what is going on. I saw this firsthand because I felt disappointed when the students weren't more enthusiastic about the changes in the sine waves when we changed the coefficients. I now realize that this was not because they weren't interested but because they did not understand what was happening.

Again, Kim includes a good suggestion for improvement: "I feel this would have been tremendously improved had I spent more time plotting points and developing a few of the other curves with them. Then, as we changed the coefficients, they would have realized why the change was occurring and therefore how it affected the curve."

Kim realizes the importance of listening to experienced people who may have more knowledge than she and shows that her beliefs regarding the essential nature of monitoring and regulating are beginning to develop:

Although I had anticipated that this class may not be ready for this lesson, I went ahead and did it anyway. My cooperating teacher had apprehensions about this lesson, and I should have worked more closely with him on adapting the lesson plan to fit the needs of these students. I should have been more prepared to deviate from this lesson and give more development to the sine curve itself.

Monitoring and Regulating.   Kim goes into more detail on how she should have improved the interactive aspects of her lesson:

Again, I believe I was so determined to pull off this lesson that I did a very poor job of monitoring and therefore regulating. I saw the loss of motivation, but I did not connect it to a loss of understanding at the time. If I had done a better job of monitoring, perhaps I would have ended up spending the entire lesson on just developing different curves on the page. But instead, I was asking the class to make conjectures on curves they did not yet understand. Live and learn!

Evaluating and Suggesting.   Not only was Kim disappointed in her lesson, but she was disappointed in her inability to accurately assess her lesson after it was over at the postlesson conference.

Although a lot of my postlesson conference evaluations were accurate, such as my questions getting better, remaining more neutral, the climate being good, as I stated earlier, I do not believe my assessment of goal achievement was accurate. I also stated my mode of representation was good, but I now see that my board work was poor, leaving much uncertainty and confusion amongst the class and students.

I was disappointed in the outcome of this lesson. I was expecting it to be so much better. I believe my biggest problem was wanting to forge ahead with a lesson they were obviously not ready to approach in the mode of representation I had planned. The biggest lesson I learned from this lesson, besides clarifying definitions and such, was learning to be ready and willing to adapt. That was the biggest downfall in this lesson. I was unwilling and unprepared to take a step back and fill in the development that they were lacking. I expected too much and did too little.

Kim learned one of the most important lessons about teaching: You must use student feedback as a means for making decisions about whether or not and how to change the course of a lesson. A common mistake among mathematics teachers is acting like a "runaway train" in an effort to cover the content, disregarding the fact that the students in the class are no longer "on the train." By using the model as a means of structuring her reflection on and assessment of the lesson, the supervisor was able to help Kim analyze her lesson in a complete and thoughtful manner.

REFLECTION AND SELF-ASSESSMENT WITH PEERS

In addition to being observed by your supervisor and cooperating teacher, there is much to be gained by engaging in observations with your peers. Because your peers are experiencing similar problems to yours, having them observe you is a powerful technique for reflecting on your own practice. That is why we suggest that you engage in at least one peer observation during your student teaching semester. Select a fellow student teacher who will observe you and whom you will observe. Use the same forms and procedures that your supervisor uses to observe you. That is, before the lesson, give your "observing peer" a copy of your prelesson thoughts and your lesson plan. After the lesson, engage in the same type of conference with your peer that you do with your supervisor. Following the conference, write your postlesson thoughts and share them with your observing peer. Submit all the forms from this peer observation experience to your supervisor. In addition, you should both write separate reports that document your reactions to the peer observation.

The following peer observation report written by Gerard reveals what he learned from observing his friend Susannah teach. The first thing Gerard noticed when observing Susannah was that watching her was somewhat like watching himself:

> I have to admit, when I first heard that we would have to do a peer observation, I thought it was a good idea, but little did I know just how great an experience it would be. As I watched Susannah work, I saw someone who was just as fresh in teaching as I was, trying all the same teaching methods that I try in my classroom also. This was the advantage of observing my peer versus observing a seasoned teacher; I was basically watching myself. It was amazing just how alike we all teach, trying to incorporate the discovery learning, cooperative learning, board work, etc., and I was able to see how it looks from the outside. I was able to see what techniques worked and which did not, and ways to improve on them. For example, I noticed that Susannah used colored chalk in her lesson, and this really inspired the class. One of the girls who went to the board (another thing Susannah did well) wrote her answer in multiple colors, changing from red to blue halfway through the answer. Though it was time-consuming, I noticed that every student in the class was paying attention as the student went over her answer. The next day I went out and bought colored chalk. I also noticed that by having students to the board often, it created a good learning environment in the class. I feel this way because the students seemed very willing to ask any questions that they had and were not hesitant to express their views on how to do the problems.

It was encouraging to note that Gerard used student involvement as a means of assessing the effectiveness of the strategies that Susannah was using.

Prior to this observation experience, Gerard was passing judgment on all student answers. To empower the students, he needed to remain neutral to student responses and let the class debate the issues. Only after Gerard observed Susannah doing the same thing, and the effects it had on her students, was he able to make the change in his own instruction. Here is what he says about it in his observation of Susannah:

I also observed the negative effects of not remaining neutral to student answers. Susannah seemed quick to praise students' answers, and though the praise was good, I noticed that on one of the questions when Susannah said "good answer," one of the other students looked at her friend and said "I have no idea." The student then asked his question, but in a class where students may be more shy, Susannah's not remaining neutral to an answer may keep students from asking a questions they have.

Gerard notes the big difference he found between watching Susannah and watching the many seasoned teachers he had observed in the past:

Susannah did a superb job teaching her class. To me, she has been able to master many of the techniques that we have been taught in our methods class, and the class responded well to her because of it. I hadn't noticed just how few teachers bring students to the board at any point during their lessons, because as I watched Susannah I felt like this was the first time I had seen many of these teaching techniques being used on such a large scale. And I have to say, I like what I saw. The students seemed so happy to be in her class. They were thrilled when they were called to the board. When they had questions, the first person they looked to for the answer was their classmates.

Again, it was refreshing to see that Gerard used student behavior as the barometer for evaluating Susannah's practice.

Gerard, indicates the powerful effect this peer observation had on him in the following statement, which incidentally, was supported by our subsequent observations of him: "Overall, I noticed that the following day I was using many of the techniques that Susannah used, and the techniques that I kept as my own that I now had more confidence in because I had seen that in action."

In his comments, Gerard has documented the many advantages that can be derived from peer observations. Somehow you are able to see yourself in your peer. This is the most objective view you may ever get of yourself, and it can be used to great advantage. According to Gerard, it enabled him to see the effects of the discourse on student learning.

We hope that you will carry the value of peer observations with you so that when you enter the teaching profession, you will continue to engage in such practices with your colleagues. A great deal happens during a lesson, and your thoughts and decisions are colored by your perception of what happens. It is always worthwhile to invite someone into your class-room to observe your lesson from a different vantage point and provide a fresh perspective of the events that transpire. A teacher who can observe your lesson from the back of the classroom is likely to see things you may not have noticed and can provide added feedback for the interactive deci-sions you make during the course of a lesson. Likewise, when you observe your colleagues' teaching, you can take a more objective perspective of the effects of certain instructional practices on student learning.

REFLECTION AND SELF-ASSESSMENT
THROUGH THE USE OF A VIDEOTAPE

Videotaping is a powerful tool that can help you develop as a teacher. Although the process of being videotaped can be threatening and viewing the tape can often be uncomfortable, the advantages are well worth it. We have found that videotaping is one of the only ways that teachers can assess the interactive nature of their instruction. That is, you can closely examine the degree to which you are monitoring what is going on in your classroom and how well you regulate your instruction accordingly. It is also one of the only ways that you can carefully assess the discourse that occurs in your class. It is for this reason that we encourage you to video-tape as many of your lessons as possible over the course of the semester. It is a good idea to make one of your first videos when your supervisor is observing you. This way you can compare what your supervisor sees with what you perceive while you are teaching and what you observe when you watch the videotape. Often student teachers claim that they did not really believe what their supervisors said until they saw it with their own eyes. From her videotape, Annie noticed a behavior she had been resistant to change:

> I learned a lot from watching my video. I saw many things that my supervisor said that I needed to improve. I did not give the students the "floor" as I should have. For example, I saw that while one of my stu-dents was at the board, I stood in the front with him. I even went so far as to redo one of his problems. I realize that I should have allowed the student to correct his work or should have allowed him to call on some-one for help.

Jackie's video helped her change her beliefs about her role in the classroom:

When I first started student teaching, I felt it imperative to be the answer woman. I took quite an authoritarian position, not because I didn't think the students capable of answering, but because I honestly thought it was my place to answer each student's question. I was not aware of the negative connotations or even that there were better ways to handle this until it was pointed out to me on my first observation and I was able to see it on the video. It was then that I decided to make this a point of self-growth.

At the end of the semester, you should make another videotape. This video serves at least two purposes. First, it allows you to document any changes you notice from your first videotape. Second, it forms the basis for independent reflection and self-assessment. That is, after at least four structured observations by your supervisor and one peer observation during the course of the semester, you should be able to assume the role of being your own supervisor. Toward that end, as part of your final self-assessment project, prepare a lesson in which you supervise yourself. Videotaping this lesson will not only help you remember what occurred during the lesson but will give you an improved perspective, more similar to that of an observer. In preparation for this lesson, complete the same forms you use when you are going to be observed by your supervisor. That is, write your prelesson thoughts and your lesson plan. After you teach your lesson and observe it on videotape, write your postlesson thoughts and complete the appropriate forms that document your analysis of the lesson. Continuing in the role as your own supervisor, you should then complete the forms that document your own assessment of your cognitions. As your own supervisor, what do you think about your goals for the lesson? What do you think about the level of knowledge you have indicated and exhibited about your students, the content, the pedagogy? How well do you think you monitored and regulated your instruction? How well do you think you were able to evaluate your lesson and make suggestions for improvement?

After completing this self-assessment project, you should have a final conference with your supervisor. Share segments of the videotape and your written work that explains why the lesson looks as it does. That is, show both what you perceive are good points and weak points of the lesson, and address the cognitions that you feel are responsible for these teaching episodes. You should stop the tape at points when you made specific decisions and explain what your thoughts were at that time. Finally, address any new knowledge you have gained or beliefs that you have changed as a result of engaging in this self-assessment process. You can also use the videotape to document any cases where evidence of change (from an earlier videotape) is clearly indicated. The directions for this final self-assessment project appear in Appendix D-7.

Students notice many things on the videotape that they never realized before. For example, Carol noticed that her listening skills were lacking:

> Another thing I did bothered me; I don't know if you can tell on the videotape, because the camera wasn't focused on me, but while the students were explaining their work at the overhead, I didn't really listen. I was walking around the room making sure everyone else was attentive, but I really didn't pay attention myself. I wasn't concerned that a mistake would go by unnoticed, I was more upset with myself that I lost track of what I was supposed to be doing. I was off task!

Lisa had been struggling with discourse since the beginning of the semester. She got into the habit of passing judgment on all student responses. She was pleased with the change she noticed on her final videotape: "As I watched my last video, I was happy to see all the long fragments where I said nothing. The students talked by themselves. They were the ones who were deciding if something was right or wrong."

Joyce also noticed an improvement from her earlier videotape:

> The tapes reveal that my questioning techniques have improved. In the beginning, I did not wait long enough for hands before calling on a student. Thus, I did not give all students a chance to ponder the questions I asked. The first video illustrates this. Further, I did not leave enough time in between each question. Fortunately, however, the second video shows how I have drastically improved in both of these areas.

Pascale also recognized the progress she had made by comparing her two videotaped lessons:

> The segment I selected from my first video is the one that shows me repeating what the student says. At the beginning of the semester, I did this a lot. In the second video, you'll see me asking students to either repeat what they said or asking them to speak up. At the beginning of the year I really didn't think it was such a big thing when I repeated what the students said. But over time, I realized that if I keep repeating the student, the other students are going to tune out when any student is speak-

ing. And since I want the students to listen to each other and respond to each other, it was important to make sure I stopped repeating them. The more I got students to answer each other's questions or sort out confusion, the more dynamic the class became. Students wanted the opportunity to explain things to their peers.

Jessica gave a convincing written testimony to the value of the videotape for improving discourse:

All semester I knew what I was having problems with, but nothing brought it home as well as this videotape. There's just something so much more understandable about the mistakes you're making and how to improve them when you actually get to see them. I know now how teacher centered I really am and that just planning to call students to the board more often doesn't fix this. It's the questions you ask and the explaining you encourage your students to do that are important. Now I see that I give the students absolutely no responsibility—I do everything for them. I also know from the video how boring and ineffective this is. My biggest problem all semester has been not knowing how to change, but I think this stemmed from not knowing how bad my discourse actually was. I now understand how much more involved I have to get every student in every lesson. The reason every student is not involved in my lessons is that I never call on anybody. This is something else that must change. If I concentrate more on calling on every student I will have to talk less and force myself to get them to explain more. This will get them actively involved in their learning, which is best for everyone!

When discussing her plans for the future Jessica added: "When I do get a job, I will have to tape my lessons frequently to monitor my discourse."

As these students have discovered, videotaping is the best way you can view the interactive nature of your instruction. It allows you to carefully examine the discourse as well as the moments in which you monitor and regulate your instruction. For this reason, if you wish to contribute to your own professional growth, continue to videotape your teaching throughout your career. It is even more helpful if you can watch the videotape with a colleague. Teaching need not be an isolated endeavor. The more communication you have with your colleagues regarding professional matters, the more rapidly you will improve.

REFLECTION AND SELF-ASSESSMENT
THROUGH JOURNAL WRITING

Most teachers will agree that a large percentage of their thoughts about teaching come to them throughout every day, outside the classroom. Using the premise that teaching can be considered a work in progress, it is important for teachers to be able to record their thoughts and feelings about what occurs in relation to their instructional practice. This process allows you to revisit the experiences and analyze them from an organized perspective. Teaching offers moments of great satisfaction and great disappointment. Writing is a vehicle through which you can express your emotions and when necessary resolve problematic situations. It is also a way for you to communicate with your supervisor and get feedback about your concerns on a daily basis. The model provides a structure through which you can reflect on and make better sense of the many teaching experiences you have. Although our students have used the journal to discuss all aspects of their cognitions and instructional practice, we have found that their most common focus is on the monitoring and regulating they do during instruction. The journal seems to provide the opportunity they need to rethink the decisions they made during the course of instruction. Many students use the journal to express concerns they have about their goals, knowledge, and beliefs. The following excerpts from student journals exemplify how student teachers have used the model to help them reflect on critical moments of their classroom practices. In addition, supervisors can raise questions and provide helpful feedback by reviewing students' journals. The examples in this section focus on the student teachers' overarching cognitions (goals, knowledge, and beliefs) and the interactive stage of their teaching (monitoring and regulating).

In her journal, Alison discusses two different types of goals she had for her students. The first goal was of a general nature. She expresses a possible conflict between the goals of her administration and her own goals. Observing a fellow teacher served as a catalyst for her thoughts on this matter:

> Today I observed one of the most organized teachers at the school. This teacher functions as a well-programmed robot. Yet, with all her great organization skills, she is a classroom dictator. There is no room for any creativity or discourse in this class, all pure mechanics. I keep on questioning myself, What makes for good teaching? Why are those who are teacher centered and dominant generally celebrated by the school

administration? Is it because their students do so well on the Regents exam? I hate Regents! I was told by some teachers that teaching for passing them must be the goal. How about teaching for understanding, or showing the beauty of mathematics?

Alison is facing the dilemma that most teachers face. Unfortunately, it is very difficult to meet the demands of a standardized exam and at the same time engage students in exciting problem-solving activities. The model has helped Alison understand that her dilemma concerns decisions about the goals she has for her students, which hinges on her beliefs about what is most important for them as learners in her class.

Alison writes about her goals for a particular lesson: "I can't say it went perfectly; however, I achieved most of my goals for this lesson. They spoke mathematics! I was able to conference with all students, I did not lose control of the class, and they solved a lot of challenging problems. I believe this lesson gave a chance to many of the students to believe in their abilities since there was a lot of tutoring in groups." From a supervisor's perspective, reading this journal entry confirms the idea that Alison's goals for her students coincide with those recommended by the reform movement. That is, along with her desire to maintain control of the class and complete her plans for the lesson, she wants them to communicate mathematically, she wants them to become problem solvers, and she wants them to become confident in their abilities.

Another student teacher, Judy, writes about her lack of knowledge, which impeded her ability to regulate her instruction: "There are times when I'd like to go back and change something, rephrase a question or complete a concept, and because I am not very comfortable teaching yet, I don't know how to handle the situation." The fact that Judy was able to verbalize her problem with monitoring and regulating demonstrates that she is indeed monitoring her instruction and is aware of the need to regulate her instruction. The supervisor uses Judy's journal entry as an opportunity to praise her for this awareness. Her admitted lack of knowledge about how to handle the situation indicates that she is motivated to learn more about what to do. Issues such as this are brought up for classroom discussion during the weekly student teaching seminar.

In addition to thinking about their own beliefs on teaching mathematics, students teachers quickly become aware that they must consider their students' beliefs as well. In the following excerpt from her journal, Yelena shows her awareness of the conflict between her beliefs and her students' beliefs and how it worked to the detriment of her lesson: "Class today was a little bumpy. I tried to have the students discover the area of a trapezoid by dividing it up into two triangles. What a flop! After the lesson, my cooperating teacher suggested that the kids just wanted to know the formula—that's all they cared about. She said that she heard one of the students say, "We don't care where it comes from—just give us the formula." Oh well, live and learn." This short journal entry was grounds for much conversation with the supervisor and Yelena, especially since her comment "live and learn" leaves one confused about how she stands on the issue. Her desire to engage the students in the derivation of the formula demonstrates that Yelena believes it is important for students to understand where a formula comes from, which was contrary to the students, who believed the only important thing to learn was the formula itself. The question for Yelena is, "Why do you think students believed that only knowing the formula is sufficient?" This conversation, of course, leads to the issue of assessment. Most students want to learn what they are expected to reproduce on their examinations. Therefore, if a teacher truly believes that understanding of formulas is important, then they should include test questions that assess their students' understanding of the derivation of the formulas.

Yelena's journal entry served as a good opportunity to discuss the connection between beliefs and assessment techniques in instructional practice.

In her journal entry, Arlene indicates how her awareness of her students' confusion and her desire to bring clarity to all of her students led her to change her lesson in ways that created more confusion:

Today was somewhat disturbing. For the first time, I experienced a disaster lesson. The object of the lesson was to derive the distance formula. I decided to let students discover the distance formula while looking at a specific case. The students had no trouble doing this. However, when the general case was introduced, I lost most of the students. Many of them showed that they didn't understand. This made me feel very uncomfortable. I didn't know what to do.

I knew that I couldn't proceed with the lesson until everyone understood. I went back to the specific case and then tried to make the connection with the general case. More students started to understand. However, I was not satisfied. I wanted the entire class to understand. So I went back to the specific case again. I noticed some students were getting bored and started to misbehave. Luckily the bell rang and my moment of horror was over. My cooperating teacher said that the best way to handle this situation is to proceed with the lesson. Eventually the ones who don't understand will pick up the concepts later after they do practice problems.

Arlene has described a situation that most teachers of mathematics encounter on a daily basis. Rarely do all of the students understand things at the same time. Arlene is to be praised for her awareness and concern that some of the students were confused and for her efforts to resolve the confusion. Although her cooperating teacher's idea to just proceed might be good advice in some cases, the issue deserves further analysis. That is, there are many other courses Arlene could have taken at the moment of confusion, as well as methods she could have used to prevent the confusion in the first place. At this point, the supervisor can help Arlene think of other tasks or teaching strategies that would have been helpful. For example, when she sensed misunderstanding she could have had the students break up into pairs and try to explain it to one another. Also, Arlene might have been able to prevent the confusion altogether by adjusting the task she created for her students. To help Arlene reflect on this matter, her supervisor might ask her how many specific cases she gave her students before asking them to make a generalization? If she merely gave them one case, then surely that would be grounds for confusion. To recognize a pattern leading to a generalization, students need a minimum of three specific cases. Arlene's journal entry served as a good opportunity for the supervisor to help Arlene recognize other options for regulating her instruction at the moment or regulating her plans for teaching that lesson another time.

People who enter teaching are often surprised by the amount of work that is required. As you well know, it entails far more than just walking into a classroom and telling students how to do mathematics. Teachers spend endless hours preparing lesson plans, homework assignments, quizzes, exams, projects, and other interesting activities. The same process you use to reflect on and assess your instructional practice should be used in relation to the written materials you create for your students. One means of documenting your work as a teacher is to assemble a portfolio. That is the focus of the next chapter.

Chapter 7

Using a Portfolio to Document How You Engage in Self-Assessment and Reflection

A portfolio is a useful tool for both professional and personal development. You can use it for professional purposes: It is not unusual to be asked for a portfolio when you apply for a teaching position, and it is required for National Board Certification. Or you may want to create a portfolio for personal use, as a means of documenting your professional growth and collecting your best pieces of work for future reference. Whatever your goal, you can use the guidelines given in this chapter for creating a portfolio.

Using the model as a conceptual basis for linking your instructional practice to your underlying cognitions, you can create a portfolio that documents your growth as a teacher. The portfolio we recommend goes far beyond a mere collection of lesson plans, homework assignments, projects, and assessment instruments. These documents have more meaning when they are accompanied by your written thoughts on what went into their creation and your reflections following their implementation. (Note that these written reflections are required for National Board Certification.) For each piece that you include in your portfolio, you should include a written rationale that explicitly states what you know about the students, the content, and methods of pedagogy and defines your goals for your students. In addition, every lesson plan, written assignment, and assessment you include should be accompanied by a written reflection on how your students reacted.

To help you better understand the types of pieces that you can include in a portfolio, this chapter presents examples from actual student teachers' portfolios. These examples are more important for the thoughts that accompany them than for the quality of the specific lesson plan, homework assignment, or assessment instrument. That is, the process of ongoing professional growth lies in your ability to know why you do what you do and to then evaluate whether or not it works effectively and how you might be able to improve its effectiveness. Teaching has often been described as a continual learning process. It is the act of learning that should be the highlight of the portfolio.

Kelly included a good description of the value and purpose of a portfolio in her portfolio overview:

> For me, this portfolio has been one long work in progress. Each day, each lesson, every class, test, and student interaction has been an extension of the last. There was always a piece of yesterday's mistake being corrected or improved on in today's lesson, and the same will hold true for every tomorrow to come. There are no perfect lessons or best ways to approach a topic. I will always be striving for the better way to accomplish student understanding, because for me this is the most important goal.

This chapter presents examples of a lesson plan, a homework assignment, a long-term project, and a quiz. Each example includes quotations from the teacher's written thoughts before and after the activity. The chapter concludes with a critique of a section of a textbook that a student teacher included in her portfolio. These particular pieces were chosen because they exemplify how the model can be used as a basis for analyzing the materials used and activities created for students. Note that portfolios should consist of many other pieces that document your work as a teacher. Some of our student teachers have included mathematical autobiographies, resumes, observation reports of other teachers, observation reports of themselves, unit plans, unit exams, alternative assessment instruments, videotapes of lessons, samples of student work, and samples of letters from students—and much more.

LESSON PLAN

Writing lesson plans is a major part of every teacher's work. The format of a plan can range from thoughts in a teacher's mind to a detailed written script for what a teacher will do and say and specific activities for students. However, regardless of the format of the plan, it contains messages about the teacher's goals, knowledge, and beliefs. These cognitions are evident in Bryan's prelesson thoughts:

> The goal of this lesson was to have the students using manipulatives "discover" the relationships of angles formed by transversal lines. I wanted to teach transversal lines using discovery learning because otherwise they would find learning the properties boring. So I found a way to allow them the chance to figure out the properties for themselves and explain them to me. I know the students love when they become the teachers and explain the properties to me. I tried to address most of the anticipated difficulties in the lesson itself. I have to make sure that I have enough time at the end of class to derive the properties from what the students had discovered.

Bryan values a student-centered approach to teaching and is aware of the interests and desires of his students. His lesson plan follows.

Topic: Angles formed by parallel lines cut by a transversal

Aim: What relationships exist between the angles formed by parallel lines cut by a transversal?

Instructional format: Individual exploration leading to a whole-class discussion

Motivational activity: Have a ruler and two pieces of pattie paper on students' desks at the start of class. Challenge the students to see if using only the given materials they can discover a set of fundamental relationship between the angles formed by parallel lines cut by a transversal.

Instructions: Using transparencies, perform each step to demonstrate.
1. Have a student define parallel lines.
2. Have all students draw a set of parallel lines separated by the width of the ruler on their pattie paper. Make sure they label their lines AB and CD.
3. Instruct students to use the ruler to draw a nonperpendicular diagonal line that crosses through both parallel lines. Label this new line EF.
4. Have the students label the angles formed from 1 though 8 as indicated on the diagram below.

5. Have the students trace what has been written on the first piece of paper onto the second.

Discovery: Students will work in pairs.
1. Ask students if just by looking at the pieces of papers they can make a conjecture regarding whether any angles have equal measures. Ask them how they can confirm their hypothesis (leads to use of pattie paper).
2. *Revision: Demonstrate how to line up different angles using the separate pieces of pattie paper.
3. Inform students that there are at least 8 sets of these relationships. Challenge them to see who can find the most.
4. Indicate that there is another relationship between some of the angles that is not that of equality. Challenge them to find it.

Final summary and conclusion:
1. Randomly select one student from each group to write on the board the relationships that their group discovered.
2. Engage students in a discussion of these relationships and arrive at a statement using the terms *alternate interior angles, corresponding angles, alternate exterior angles,* and *interior angles on the same side of the transversal.*

Bryan's postlesson thoughts indicate that this lesson proceeded quite well and, in Bryan's estimation, needed only slight adjustment. His comments show that he was able to address the concepts planned for the lesson and at the same time capture the interest and understanding of the students. Very often teachers find that their greatest challenge is to cover the content and achieve student understanding all in one lesson.

This plan did proceed as I had expected. The students were able to derive every property in a very short amount of time. Once they discovered that the pattie paper could be flipped around it was easy for them to find the angles with equal measure. To my surprise, three of the students in the class were able to come up with the supplementary angles. When I observed this lesson being taught in another class using a teacher-centered method of just telling students the properties, I found the students were quite bored and uninterested. I was glad to see that my class responded with a high level of enthusiasm. The only problem I had was that in the original plan, I had not prepared for them to not understand how to use the pattie paper to determine which angles have equal measure. That is why I inserted a question in my revised lesson plan to demonstrate this. I will use this method of teaching this lesson again in the future, for it not only uses discovery learning but it also suggests to the students that these properties work every time (because each student had different angles formed and yet they all came to the same conclusions).

Bryan's assessment of his lesson is based on his analysis of the interest and involvement of his students.

HOMEWORK ASSIGNMENT

Most teachers agree that homework is a critical part of the teaching-learning process. Learning mathematics necessitates active involvement on the students' part. Giving students problems to do on their own in the privacy of their homes affords them the opportunity to practice what they have learned, to discover what it is they do not understand, and possibly to extend their learning through new applications. In addition to thoughtfully assigning problems from the text, teachers should try to assign interesting problems by consulting other sources and or using their own creativity. The following homework assignment was created by Jeannette to alert students to common mistakes they make. Jeanette describes the assignment as follows:

The homework assignment referred to here consisted of 15 algebraic problems that represented a fictional quiz taken by a fictional student. The homework assignment required the students to make corrections to the fictional student's work. The following directions were given:

Mrs. Tuttle gave the following problems as a quiz to her Regents class. Below are the solutions given by her student, Pat Mathlover. She needs your help correcting this quiz. Each solution has at least one error in it. Determine where Pat made mistakes, and give the correct solution to each problem. Then write an explanation for why you corrected the problems as you did. For every 3 problems you properly correct and explain, Mrs. Tuttle will give you an extra point on your upcoming exam (for a possible total of 5 extra points).

One of the examples on the test was as follows:

Problem: Reduce $x^2 + 2x - 3 / (x^2 + 3x)$ to lowest terms.

Pat's work:

$$\frac{(x+3)(x+1)}{x(x+3)} = \frac{(x+3)(x+1)}{x(x+3)} = \frac{x+1}{x} = \frac{x+1}{x} = 1$$

Corrections:

Explanations:

This is Jeannette's rationale for creating this homework assignment:

The assignment includes 15 problems representative of the topics covered for algebraic fractions. The students are to mark the answers provided by a fictional student. The incorrect solutions include some obvious and not-so-obvious mistakes that my students tend to make. Hopefully, by recognizing the errors in this manner, the students will better digest them. For each problem, a corrected solution is required, along with a detailed written explanation (using appropriate mathematical reasoning). Requiring the students to communicate the math should hopefully reinforce their knowledge of it. Since it is really a homework assignment, the point values given are not extremely large, but nonetheless the motivation is there and it will help the students study.

Jeannette's comments reveal much about her goals, knowledge, and beliefs. First, by creating the problems, she demonstrates that she is aware of the common errors and areas of misunderstandings of her students. She appears to believe that having students see the errors made by others will help them understand the concepts better. By requiring students to provide written explanations, it is clear that her goal is to have students communicate mathematically because she believes that this is a means for improving their learning. Finally she reveals her goal of creating an assignment that will be motivational for the students, based on her belief that motivation is an aid for getting students to study.

In her postassignment reflections, Jeannette reveals her disappointment:

I thought this assignment was a great idea, as did some of the teachers I showed it to where I student teach. However, my students found it extremely difficult. Perhaps this is because I made the errors match the typical mistakes they tend to make. Many of them wrote only brief explanations of the corrections, if any at all. I think my students still have this fear of writing about math, or rather a confusion about it. They seem to be able to only write about the procedural aspects of mathematics. I am trying to get them to go deeper than this.

Out of a possible total of 5 extra credit points, the average granted was a mere 1. Many students did not even complete the review sheet (which is unacceptable since it was a homework assignment). A few students got 4 or 5 points, but most of the students just tried to do the minimal amount of work. The feedback and comments I received were that it was very hard, although some admitted that it was a good idea. I had expected much better results and for it to be met with greater enthusiasm. I think the problem is that these students are not so accustomed to change or variety. I know they like it though, it just takes some getting used to.

By reflecting on her students' performance and reactions to this assignment, Jeannette has learned more about her students and how she is beginning to form new beliefs. She recognizes that her students fear writing and change and that they only focus on procedures. However, she recognizes that the students like the idea of something different. Therefore, rather than reverting back to the usual types of assignments, Jeannette is determined to keep pushing the students to engage in activities that she feels will improve their learning.

LONG-TERM PROJECT

Another type of homework assignment is a long- term project. Projects can be a wonderful motivator for students, especially those who are disinterested in mathematics. Projects can give students the chance to learn about mathematics and engage in mathematical problem solving. We encourage our student teachers to design at least one interesting project for their students. In line with the model, they must explain the thoughts that went into their design of the project and then they must use the students' work as a means for assessing and reflecting on the quality of the project design.

The following project, created by Stella, is highlighted here not because the assignment itself was so innovative or successful but because of the quality of her cognitions with regard to the assignment.

The project Stella assigned to her precalculus students was to count 20% of the final grade. She gave them a choice of three topics: Exponential Growth, Sports Statistics, and Masters of Math. For each topic, she included a thorough description. To summarize, the Exponential Growth project required the students to estimate how the world's population would grow in 50 years. The Sports Statistics project required the students to select two professional players or teams and compare the historical performance statistics over the years. The Masters of Math project required the students to choose a mathematician and write about his or her life, contribution to mathematics, and discoveries. Whichever topic they picked, students were given the following instructions: "You should use as many mathematical tools as possible, such as charts, graphs, tables, and so on. You have to use information from books or from the Internet. You must list your sources in the last page of your paper." They were told that their grade would be based on "content, creativity, use of mathematical tools, and oral presentation."

In her written rationale for this project, Stella states, "When I was constructing the project assignment for my class, I tried to find a topic that is related to precalculus. I also wanted a topic that would attract my students' interest, so the project would be a fun assignment for them, especially since my students had never been asked to do a math project." Stella focuses on her students, and her goals are both cognitive and affective. She wants them to learn something related to precalculus and she wants them to enjoy it.

Stella next describes her rationale for each of the three choices: "All the topics that I researched were great topics for projects, but they were suitable for either lower-level students or calculus students. Exponential Growth was the only topic that I could think of that was related to what we had learned in class. I thought this topic could be slightly difficult. However, I put it as part of the choices because there might be some students that would like to do research on it." Stella's comments reveal her concern for choosing a task that is at the appropriate level of difficulty for her students.

Stella also describes her rationale for choosing the sports topic: "I was confident that a project on sports would draw many of my students' interest since some of them belong to a sport team in the school." This comment shows that Stella has knowledge of both her students' interests as well as their involvements.

Finally, this is Stella's reason for choosing the topic about mathematicians: "For the other topics, students have to use a great deal of statistics. Thus, I wanted something different for the third topic. Some of my students are good in English, and they do not see math as a fascinating subject." Stella's goal to hook students into appreciating mathematics is clearly evident in this remark.

Stella's respect for her students and knowledge of her students' needs are evident in the process she used to help students begin their work on the project:

> I made sure that this assignment was ready to be given out before the winter break, so students would have enough time to work on it. I prepared a sheet that they had to fill out with their chosen topic, sources, questions, and time of free period. Writing a topic and sources would pressure them to start working on this assignment right away. The questions that students may write would help me see what needs to be clarified about this project. I wanted to know when are my students' free periods in case I found it necessary to meet with them individually later on.

By giving the students adequate time to do the project and by scheduling meetings at the students' convenience, Stella establishes a respectful social and intellectual climate with her class. In addition, by giving the students opportunities to ask questions about the assignment, Stella demonstrates her desire to monitor and regulate the students' work on this project.

Much to Stella's surprise, most of the students did the project: "Surprisingly, a huge amount of students handed in the project. Only three students did not hand in their projects. One of these students told me that he had to finish it when I asked him about it. However, a few days passed and he did not hand it in. A day before the project was due many students came to me and asked me for an extra day, so I gave it to the whole class. By extending the deadline, Stella again demonstrates her flexible position and kind attitude towards her students.

Stella's kindness perhaps was overextended in her grading, which she describes as follows: "Since I wanted this to be a good experience for the students, I did not want to be too strict grading the papers. Thus, most students got A's, a few got B's, and only one student got C+ because he just printed a table from the Internet as his paper. Certainly, those students who did not do the project received F's." Although Stella's grading policy can certainly be debated, the point taken here is that Stella was consistent with her original goal for students that they appreciate mathematics.

The work Stella did on her postproject assessment reveals a few issues Stella needs to think about. Contrary to the detail of her preproject comments, her postproject comments are rather general and never discuss in detail the quality of work the students produced. As she becomes more experienced, she might revisit her decision to count this one project as such a high percentage of the grade if she is going to be so generous with her marks. She also might revisit her criteria and figure out a more detailed rubric to use when grading the work.

QUIZ

Quizzes and exams are integral parts of the teaching-learning process. When teachers create assessment instruments, they must have clearly defined rationales for what they require students to do. Kaye created the following quiz question:

1. State the distance and midpoint formulas.
2. Jack just learned the distance and midpoint formulas. He was assigned the following problem: ABCD is a parallelogram. Its vertices have the following coordinates: A(–6,8), B(2,10), C(6,4), D(–2,2). M, N, L, and O are the midpoints of sides AD, AB, DC, and BC, respectively. What kind of quadrilateral is MNLO?
3. Jack's sister Ann is in seventh grade and loves geometry. She looked at the graph and suggested that MNLO is a parallelogram. Prove or disprove Ann's assumption. Show all your work.

In her rationale, Kaye states:

As I constructed this instrument, I had several objectives in mind. I wanted to check, first, whether the students know the formulas of distance and midpoint and if they can apply them. Secondly, their reading comprehension, that is, if they can read the problem and understand what is given and what they have to do to find the information or prove it. Third, to improve the students' critical thinking skills, that is, let them choose a correct assumption and carry out an argument. Using such proofs gives students a good opportunity to review the definitions of a parallelogram, a rhombus, a rectangle, and a square and to see the relationships among them.

Beyond wanting her students to merely solve the problem, Kaye understands the necessity for them to engage their reading comprehension and understanding. Kaye demonstrates her own knowledge of the question and the underlying skills that are needed to solve the problem.

In her post-quiz reflections, Kaye states:

> The quiz was graded on a 10-point scale. Knowledge of each formula was worth 1 point. Another 8 points were distributed between identifying the problem, being able to choose the correct assumption, and carrying out a proof.

> Since I evaluated the reading comprehension in the beginning of the semester, I was able to see that many of the students made significant progress. The grades ranged from 5 to 10. The average was 7.8. Students' problem-solving abilities increased. Many of them were able to apply Polya's steps for problem solving: identify the problem, derive a plan, carry out the plan, go back and justify the solution.

Kaye's post-quiz reflections show that she places a higher value on process than on product. The rubric she used for grading the exam and the way she describes how the students performed on the exam reveal that she is committed to helping the students in both their reading comprehension and on their problem-solving abilities.

CRITIQUE OF A SECTION OF A TEXTBOOK

Considering the fact that textbooks are the main sources that teachers use when constructing their lessons, it is important that teachers assess them carefully. The reflective processes they use on the activities they create for their students should be extended to the materials they use with students that others have created, specifically textbook writers. Marion not only found weaknesses in the section of the text she was using, but she designed a worksheet for her students that would compensate for these weaknesses. Here is her description of the text's section on inverse functions:

> When it comes to sequencing and promoting student discovery, the text is really awful. There is no room for student discovery, and it is very hard to read. The material is just presented, rather than leading the student to it before stating it clearly. There are only 3 examples and their solutions in the section, and 2 of them are of the same type, while the exercises require the student to solve at least 5 different types of problems, which the book doesn't model for them.

Marion clearly understands that the way tasks are sequenced has pedagogical implications. Her comments also reveal that she believes it is important for students to discover new concepts on their own. What was most impressive was that Marion took the time and effort and had the knowledge of how to improve the textbook. She writes, "I have constructed and attached a group worksheet which promotes student discovery by having them do simple review type exercises and then examine the results in order to derive the properties of inverse functions." Marion's approach is to have one person in a group doing one set of problems and another person in the group doing another set of related problems. After they finish, she asks them to compare their results to come up with a conclusion. For example, in one case, she has two people create different graphs of a function and its inverse and asks them, "Examine both graphs, and the relationship between the graphs of each function and its inverse. From these examples, can you notice a special property about the graphs of pairs of inverse functions? What do you notice? Why do you think this happens?" The guided discovery worksheet that Marion has created integrates her knowledge of sequencing as well as pedagogy with a goal for student-centered instruction.

Marion shows her sensitivity to the modes of representation the textbook promotes when she says, "The text doesn't promote the use of technology at all. This is unfortunate because a graphing calculator is really helpful to demonstrate the fact that inverse functions are reflections of each other in the line $y = x$. Even something as simple as tracing paper and/or the projector can enhance a lesson in discovery of the graphs of functions and their inverses." Her reference to the use of a graphing calculator, tracing paper, and transparencies for an overhead projector show that Marion has a good understanding of which representations would facilitate students' discovery of the properties of inverses. Again, she demonstrates how she has integrated her knowledge of the content, her knowledge of modes of representation, and her knowledge of content pedagogy, all with the goal of empowering students to become independent learners.

Finally, Marion reveals her sensitivity to the types of questions that were asked in the textbook, noticing that it rarely provides occasion for students to explain any of their ideas:

> The text promotes student writing minimally, but hardly models examples for them. Rather than having an example of an "explain" question and a good answer, these types of questions are rare and only appear at the very end of the exercises, as "challenge exercises." In my group worksheet, there are some examples of opportunities for student writing as part of describing what properties they've discovered about inverse functions.

Indeed, Marion's worksheet included several opportunities for students to explain their results.

So far, this book has presented practical methods for observing and analyzing lessons, both yours and others, and techniques for documenting your learning and your experiences. This approach entails a great deal of reflection, introspection, and hard work. You certainly have the right to question whether this approach really works. The next chapter provides the evidence. It describes case studies in which we have documented the impact of this approach on the teacher preparation of some of our students.

EVIDENCE: THE MODEL IN ACTION

Chapter 8

Case Studies of the Model in Action: Five Cases

The fundamental premise of this book is that teachers' classroom practices as well as their underlying cognitions must be student centered for students to learn mathematics with understanding. In the preceding chapters, we described the development and use of our model as a way to better understand and appreciate the complexity of student-centered teaching. This chapter consists of five case studies that show various issues and concerns that arise when student teachers engage in the process of reflection and self-assessment about their cognitions and instructional practices. We created the following categories to organize student teachers' experiences and promote professional growth: Identifying the Problem, Owning the Problem and Searching for Resolution, and Growth in Self-Understanding. In addition, we include a Commentary section to share our own analysis of student teachers' experiences and to suggest probable trajectories for their progress in becoming student-centered professionals. As you read the comments of these student teachers, watch for the unspoken contradictions in what they say and what they do; feel their emotional struggles as they try to make their practice consistent with their cognitions; and share in their breakthrough moments when they confront and seek resolution of acknowledged problems. In shadowing their experiences, you get a glimpse of the complexity of the dynamic interplay between goals, knowledge, and beliefs and classroom practice and an appreciation of what it takes to grow in self-understanding of one's own teaching.

THE CASE OF MARIA: HOW KNOWLEDGE
AND BELIEFS AFFECT DISCOURSE

Maria's use of the model helped her change her questioning style from overusing chorus responses to calling on individual students and thereby increased the level of student involvement in her classes. The reflective writing required by the model helped Maria to explicitly identify the contradictions between the advice of her cooperating teacher and that of her college supervisor. The writing forced her to confront the conflicts between what she felt comfortable doing and what she was learning about questioning techniques in her college course. Furthermore, the model helped her acknowledge that her conflict was between her knowledge and her beliefs. When she considered the fact that chorus responses filtered out wrong answers and only allowed her to hear correct answers, she recognized that her beliefs about the value of chorus responses had to be reconsidered.

Maria could be described as a self-made woman. She received most of her high school education in Puerto Rico, and despite her later-recognized gift for mathematics, she graduated with few credits in the subject. She came to the United States with three children, no husband, no job, and little money, but with a strong desire to learn and to attend college. After getting A+'s in several mathematics courses, her desire to teach mathematics emerged. "I knew that with my math background, I wanted to teach kids. I am a young Puerto Rican mother whose been there, done that, and I'm good at math. I hope I can reach some of these New York City kids in ways other teachers cannot." It was clear from the start that Maria's focus was connecting to her students. At the beginning of the semester, Maria wrote in her journal that she "was very nervous and scared of how the class would take to me." It is interesting to see how her concerns about her relationship with her students influenced the nature and quality of her discourse with them, which may have negatively impacted their learning.

Identifying the Problem

In the first visit from the supervisor, Maria conducted what might be called a "chalk and talk" lesson. In keeping with that, the only questioning technique she used was to ask a question and then accept the answer that the whole class called out—the chorus response.

Owning the Problem and Searching for a Resolution

In her written postlesson thoughts and after conferencing with her supervisor, Maria understood why the chorus response was not the best approach: "I was told that the chorus responses had to go. I was so happy to be getting so many good responses that I wasn't even concerned over this. But I realize that some students are being left out. This will be another goal of mine; to get the kids to not call out!" Although, she specified this as her goal, she did not explain how she was going to accomplish it. That is, she gave no specific plans for how to prevent the students from calling out their answers. In response to Maria's postlesson thoughts, the supervisor requested that she think about a definite strategy for inhibiting students from calling out. Not surprisingly, in her second observation two weeks later, the chorus response was still evident. In her prelesson thoughts, Maria again made no mention of her plans for changing her questioning techniques. At the postlesson conference, Maria was aware that the students were still calling out, but as she later explained in her postlesson thoughts:

> I was not aware of how many questions I answered myself or the way I led the class into giving me the answers I wanted. I was not aware of how many students were being left out of the lesson because of the chorus responses . . .. At first I didn't believe, really, that chorus responses were always wrong. My cooperating teacher does it and I thought, I'm glad someone is responding. I now feel this is wrong, and I'm not just saying this. I know that as a result of chorus responses some students are laying back and not participating because there is no need to.

Maria's postlesson thoughts for her second observation included a method for how she would eliminate the chorus responses:

> Before asking a question, I will tell the class to raise their hands. I will raise my hand and I will respond to those students who have raised their hands. I also will try to wait after I ask a question so that the class has time to think about it, and hopefully I'll see more hands and new hands. Also, on some days I am going to concentrate on calling on certain areas of the class so that as I alternate areas, all students will be involved.

Maria's specific ideas for ways to change her questioning style convinced the supervisor that the next observation would reveal a change. And sure enough, there was.

Although Maria did not mention anything about changing her discourse in the prelesson thoughts of her third observation, her supervisor noted a big change in her instructional practice. In fact, she did all that she said she planned to do in the postlesson thoughts of her previous lesson. That is, before asking a question, she reminded the students to raise their hands before answering. As a reminder to students, after asking a question, she would raise her own hand. In her postlesson thoughts, she revealed what was impeding her efforts to change and what finally convinced her of the need to put an end to the chorus response. Apparently, her cooperating teacher was supporting her use of the chorus response.

> The cooperating teacher stated to me how we are just content with the fact that the class is responding and not to worry about it. As a new teacher, that hit the nail on the head for me. I was so happy the class was answering my questions that I didn't want to stop. Besides, my cooperating teacher teaches this way all the time. So, I decided, why change something that was going so well?

Maria then shared with another student how in her observations she kept being told to eliminate the chorus response and how she was reluctant to do it. The student's response made a big impression on Maria, who related the story as follows: "Then one day I was speaking to another student teacher. I told her what had happened at my conference after the observation and about my decision that I was happy that at least the kids were responding to me. She then asked, 'So you only hear the right answers?' This really made me think. Did she have a point? Was I only listening to the answers that I wanted to hear?"

Growth in Self-Understanding

In evaluating her learning experiences, Maria commented on the impact the supervisor made when confronting her true beliefs about encouraging chorus responses from her students:

> At the conference, the supervisor saw right through my BS about having to change my chorus responses. She knew I really wasn't going to try to change this because I really didn't believe yet that I had to. She

opened my eyes some more. I saw how chorus responses only cheated the students from actually learning. I have since tried to change the chorus response in my classes. But one major hurdle that I still have is that I only observe my cooperating teacher and am with her all the while I am at school. See, she has chorus response in her class all the time and I get used to hearing it to the point that I don't notice it unless I remember to.

Commentary

Through the use of the model, the supervisor was able to help Maria work through the contradictions between her knowledge and her beliefs about best pedagogical approaches. Furthermore, by putting these issues in writing, Maria was able to alert the supervisor to the contradictory messages she was getting from her cooperating teacher and the supervisor. Through Maria's writing, the supervisor was able to help her focus on the most important question: When the children were responding in chorus, how was it contributing to their learning? Only if she truly believed that most students were not getting the chance to think and that the wrong answers were going unnoticed would she be able to accomplish the difficult task of changing a routine that was set for her by the cooperating teacher.

After experiencing such extensive focus on this problem and with the clear awareness she exhibited, it is reasonable to expect that when Maria is no longer under the guidance of her cooperating teacher, she will blossom into the student-centered teacher she wants to be.

THE CASE OF IRIS: DIFFICULTY IN MONITORING AND REGULATING INSTRUCTION

Iris's use of the model helped her change from being unresponsive to student input to conducting lessons that were dependent on student input. The writing activities required by the model served as a vehicle through which she could acknowledge her own insecurities about deviating from her lesson plan. The structured postlesson conferences and postlesson written reports enabled her to articulate a compelling rationale for using student input as a means for understanding the thinking of her students, which served as her motivation to overcome her difficulties with what she called "thinking on her feet."

Iris had worked in finance for several years before deciding to be a teacher. She was overwhelmed by fear when she first began student teaching. Here is what she wrote in her journal toward the end of the semester:

> I think I felt that way because the shock was considerable. My expectations of doing well from day one were high. I had wonderful training, knowledge of math, love of children and learning, with good human relation skills. There should have been no reason why I wouldn't walk in and be a good teacher from the beginning. I did not account for the nerves, the stage fright, questioning, and the idea of thinking on your feet. I mistakenly thought these and many more aspects of teaching would be second nature to me.

As it turned out, Iris's neglect of this very important concept in teaching, thinking on your feet, contributed in no small way to her early difficulties in the classroom.

Identifying the Problem

Observation of the first lesson by the supervisor revealed that Iris tended to ignore students' incorrect answers. During the postlesson conference, the supervisor discussed with her the importance of monitoring student understanding and regulating her instruction during the course of the lesson—thinking on your feet. In the second observation, there was still no change in Iris's classroom behavior. She continued to ignore student input. Again, during the postlesson conference, the supervisor made a point of stressing the need to monitor student understanding by carefully listening to students' ideas and regulating the instruction accordingly.

Owning the Problem and Searching for Resolution

This time the postlesson conference made an impact on Iris, as she admitted in her postlesson thoughts that, "I also need to value students' ideas more and to follow their ideas and not mine. An example of this was when Annie asked to show what she found on line symmetry, I showed them what I found instead. When students came up with their own ideas, I was reluctant to go with them. Partly because of my insecurities and partly because I am afraid to go off the beaten track of my lesson plans."

During the third observation, Iris began encouraging students to express their ideas, whether they were correct or not. In fact, she designed a lesson on the intersections of loci that was totally dependent on student input. She told students that they were to embark on a treasure hunt in the classroom. Students were required to work in small groups, draw diagrams on the blackboard, and come up with different ideas for where the treasure was hidden. Contrary to her other lessons, in this lesson plan she indicated how the main ideas would come from the students. In the development section, she wrote, "Have a student come to the blackboard to draw the diagram of the room . . .. Break students into groups and then have one student from the group come up and explain how to do the problem . . .. Have a student summarize how to find the intersection of loci." In her written postlesson reflections, she indicated her commitment to understanding the thinking of her students: "I should have had the student come to the board to explain her work. First because the other students would be able to hear the student more clearly. Then second because the student is the better person to explain how they came to the conclusion than I am at guessing how the student was thinking. It also encourages the student to become more of an active member of the class."

Growth in Self-Understanding

By the end of the semester, Iris herself noticed how much she had improved her interactive classroom behaviors. In her last postlesson written comments, she noted how she monitored the understanding of one student to gauge how to proceed with the lesson. She said, "Rosemarie said she didn't understand. Rosemarie has strong math skills and is also a very conscientious student. So when she didn't understand part of the problem, I knew that other students might have had the same problem. In addition, her question pertained to a concept, not a procedure. At this time, I introduced a new and simpler problem aimed at clarifying the concept."

In her final evaluation of herself, Iris indicated that she still needed to focus on the interactive aspects of her teaching. She explained, "I am aware of the continued need for growth and development. The value of students' ideas and thoughts, by listening to them and refining their ideas instead of imposing mine are all elements of my style I need to develop."

Commentary

As Iris noted in her final reflection, "thinking on your feet," or as we would say, the interactive aspect of teaching, "is a critical aspect of good instruction." During a lesson, teachers must continuously assess the understanding of their students to regulate their instruction in ways that will meet their needs. The fact that Iris became aware of and was able to apply these cognitive strategies in the classroom with consistency indicates that she is well on her way to becoming a student-centered professional.

THE CASE OF MINDY: HOW BELIEFS AFFECT MOTIVATIONAL TASKS

As a result of using the model, Mindy improved her motivational activities from being mere attention-getters to questions that would be of interest to her low-ability students and sustain their desire to learn throughout the lesson. After several unsuccessful attempts to convince her that the tasks she created were not sufficiently motivating for her students, Mindy revealed a clue to her reluctance to change her practice in her postlesson reflections. It appeared that she believed that her choice of tasks provided the kind of motivation that was appropriate for what she felt was a "low-level class." Using the model, Mindy was able to get to the root of her problem: her incomplete knowledge of the meaning of motivation and her beliefs regarding low-ability students.

Mindy entered student teaching after teaching at a religious school for three years. She felt that teaching mathematics would be an easy transition to make. At the end of the semester, she expressed this in her journal: "At the very beginning of the student teaching semester, I thought teaching mathematics would be a breeze. All you had to do was write a lesson, carry it out, and give and grade tests. I felt since I had been teaching for three years, that carrying out the lesson would be simple. I was confident that I felt comfortable in front of the class." Mindy's rather simplistic notions about teaching belied more serious issues concerning her beliefs about students and the effect these beliefs had on their motivation to learn.

Identifying the Problem

In her first observed lesson, Mindy created the following problem for students:

> I went to the doctor last week and he said I need to be on a diet and am
> only allowed to have 130 calories for breakfast. This morning I had an

English muffin with butter. I know that they totaled 130 calories, but I don't know how many calories are in each of them. For some reason the labels don't tell me the amount, but I need to figure it out! The muffin has $300/x$ calories and the butter has $180/2x$ calories. All I know is that together they total 130 calories, but how many calories does the muffin have and how many calories does the butter have?

Although the problem started off sounding realistic, the algebraic expressions were not based on anything meaningful, and the students were given no reason to want to solve this problem. During the first post-lesson conference, the supervisor discussed with Mindy the role of motivation in student learning with understanding and how her choice of the problem was unlikely to sustain student attention and interest.

It was clear from her written postlesson comments that Mindy's ideas about motivation changed only minimally: "I believe that the muffin story was appropriate for this low-level class. It was an attention-getter—which is something they need (especially at 7:30 a.m.). For a regular class or an honors class, this story would be inappropriate, as it does not have mathematical validity. Instead, a real-life-related problem, perhaps using conversions, would be more appropriate." Mindy's comments indicate that she has made a distinction between motivation for low-ability versus high-ability students. In her opinion, meaningless attention-getters are sufficient for "low-level" students.

Mindy's attention-getting approach for low-ability students persisted in her next lesson. In her prelesson thoughts, she wrote: "This class is a low-level class, so the raisin activity should be a good motivational activity for them. They will enjoy it and have fun!" Her deficient understanding of motivation was reflected in the lesson, which had the students counting raisins in a box to learn how to use the stem-and-leaf plot. Although the materials in this lesson did capture students' interest, their true motivational potential was not realized. In the raisin lesson, instead of having students recognize the need to organize data and the value of the stem-and-leaf plot as an easy means of organizing the data, Maria had the students read off the numbers in numerical order and then she plotted them.

Once again, the supervisor discussed with Mindy the weak motivation of the lesson and how she may need to reexamine her beliefs about why she thinks motivation is different for low-ability students. This time an impression appeared to have been made.

Owning the Problem and Searching for Resolution

In her postlesson comments, Mindy surmised that a weak motivation might have contributed to only partial fulfillment of her goals:

> My goals for this lesson were for the students to understand the need for a stem-and-leaf plot, be able to make one and read one. Not all of my goals were accomplished. We never discussed any advantages to the stem-and-leaf- plot. Why did we need to learn this? I should have created a need to organize the data. While all the numbers were up on the board in no particular order, I should have asked, What is the mode? This would have created some need for organization of the data.

At this point, the supervisor felt more confident that Mindy was gaining a better understanding that motivation goes far beyond mere attention getting.

Growth in Self-Understanding

By the last lesson that Mindy was observed teaching, she demonstrated an improved understanding of motivation. Her lesson involved an extension of the positive integers to the negative integers. In this lesson, although she still used hands-on materials—a long rope that acted as a number line—she focused more attention on creating a motivational question. The problem she presented to students was, "The weather in Alaska in January was –20 degrees Fahrenheit. The next day it was –25 degrees Fahrenheit. Did the temperature get warmer or cooler?"

In her postlesson conference, Mindy was able, on her own, to point out the value of her motivational question. She said that it worked fairly well because at the beginning of the class, the students debated which day was warmer and by the end of the class, when they returned to the question, they felt satisfied that they had resolved the issue. The supervisor reinforced her satisfaction with the motivation, and Mindy revisited the issue again in her written postlesson thoughts: "The lesson started out with the motivational activity. I had a good motivational question and it was good that I got back to it. I was very happy that this lesson had a good motivational activity. I have had trouble with the actual motivation in the past, but this lesson shows my improvement."

In her self-evaluation, Mindy again noted the change in her understanding of the role of motivation in student learning:

Throughout the semester, I have been working hard to correct my weaknesses. The hardest one to correct was my lack of motivation. I finally am getting better at it! I understand the need for all lessons to be motivating. I understand what motivation is. I even understand how to incorporate motivation into a lesson. In my video observation, I had the 5 questions on the board that the students did not know how to solve. This was a void in their knowledge, and therefore the students were motivated to use the chips to solve these problems.

Commentary

Mindy's understanding of the relationship between student knowledge and motivation improved significantly. By the end of the semester, she recognized that toys and silly stories are inadequate methods of motivation for any students, regardless of their ability levels. Providing that she has no other hidden beliefs about low-ability students, she will continue to deepen her understandings of the complexities of motivation for student learning.

THE CASE OF ELIZABETH: HOW GOALS AFFECT THE LEARNING ENVIRONMENT

Elizabeth's use of the model helped her to slow down her fast-paced method of instruction, giving her students a chance to think, and giving herself a chance to understand their thinking. In the first postlesson conference, Elizabeth's supervisor asked her to assess whether or not she had accomplished the goals for student understanding that she had outlined in her prelesson thoughts. Recognizing that because she rushed the lesson she had limited student input and was unable to assess student understanding, she began to realize that her instructional practice needed changing. Through her postlesson thoughts, Elizabeth was able to articulate the necessity of reconsidering her goals for content coverage as a means of creating a learning environment that would support her goals for student understanding.

As a teaching assistant in college, Elizabeth would simply go over homework problems that the students had difficulty doing. Elizabeth explained how she used to rush through explanations to students so that she could cover as many problems as possible in the allotted time. This

experience might have contributed to the early difficulties she encountered during student teaching.

Identifying the Problem

In observing Elizabeth's first lesson, the supervisor noticed its very fast
pace. Elizabeth pushed things along by constantly saying, "Right? It's logical," and then moving on. During the postlesson conference, the supervisor asked Elizabeth to reevaluate her use of time and consider the benefits
of allowing students to investigate incorrect answers.

Owning the Problem and Searching for Resolution

The discussion during the postlesson conference had a big impact on Elizabeth's thinking, as she revealed in her written postlesson thoughts: "One
weak point of the lesson was that it was too rushed. I always feel like I am
on a timed schedule. Now I see that I can rush all I want, but if the students don't understand, it was wasted time anyway. When I sat back later
and thought about it, I realized that they were not ready for the proof at the
end. I guess I was trying to fit in too much, and this caused a problem."
Based on these comments, the supervisor felt quite certain that the pacing
in Elizabeth's next lesson would be noticeably slower. And so it was.

Growth in Self-Understanding

In her next lesson, Elizabeth slowed down the pace of her lesson by allowing time to get adequate feedback from the students and meet their learning needs. Her recognition of the importance of the relationship between
use of time and student learning was also evidenced in her prelesson
thoughts:

> My goal for the lesson was for the students to understand the ratios that
> exist in the right triangles and how useful they can be in solving prob-
> lems. I was hoping to try and introduce it in a way in which they would-
> n't forget. I know that the students love to be involved and up and
> around, so I was hoping that by having them role play being the angles
> of the triangle that they would get involved and have some fun. I figured
> that I would try to introduce it slowly, as I need to be gradual with the

preparatory classes when I teach them new things. I see a possible difficulty with getting the sides confused, which is why I want to spend a lot of time making sure they understand the differences. I am using this day to solely introduce the ratios, and am fairly sure that I will be able to fit in most of my lesson. If I have to sacrifice some of the examples so that they are clear on the ratios, then I will, as their understanding of the ratios is crucial to their success in trig.

In her subsequent lessons, Elizabeth sustained her slower-paced instruction. In her postlesson comments, she again made specific reference to her pacing and was pleased that she gave sufficient time for students to answer questions. In addition, she noticed the connection between pacing and monitoring student understanding: "I could see by the looks on their faces if they understood or not, so I had to modify the length of time we spent up there until I was able to see all students were comprehending. I spent a little longer up there than I wanted to. However, it was necessary in order to make sure all students got it."

In her final self-evaluation at the end of the semester, Elizabeth commented on her improvement once more:

I know that at the beginning of the semester, I really moved at a quick pace; however, I still wanted the students to learn, and wanted to help them. I soon realized after being observed and from [my supervisor's and cooperating teacher's] comments that I can go as fast as I want, but if they are not learning, then I am wasting my time altogether. I also would want a response to a question right away at the beginning of the semester, however now I tend to ask a question to a student, and then just sit on a desk, or something else that will keep me from jumping down their throats. I also have used the "1–Mississippi, 2–Mississippi" method. These are the ways that I keep myself from having too short of a wait time.

Commentary

Elizabeth learned one of the most important lessons about teaching for understanding and made the change to slower-paced student-centered teaching.

THE CASE OF KYUNGSO: HOW BELIEFS AFFECT CLASSROOM PRACTICE

Kyungso's use of the model helped him change from a transmission approach to one that promoted more student involvement. The model gave Kyungso many chances to explicitly confront his deeply held beliefs regarding the right way to teach. Having learned mathematics in China, Kyungso was convinced that teaching is synonymous with telling and that learning is synonymous with listening. It was difficult for him to come to terms with the inherent contradiction between his stated goals for his students and his instructional practice. However, through the constant reflection and self-assessment required by the model, Kyungso explicitly identified early signs of change in his interactions with students he was tutoring.

Kyungso had been a computer programmer and made a career change into teaching. His beliefs about teaching mathematics were consistent with a transmission view of learning, as is evidenced in his journal writing at the end of the student teaching semester:

> At the beginning of the student-teaching semester, my perception of teaching mathematics was rather naïve. I thought that all you needed to do was to think of an interesting problem to get the students motivated in the beginning. Then, just present the lesson pretty much as the textbook has it written. I was imagining that the students were attentive and ask questions. I love to deal with children, and I love to be the one to provide the correct answers. I had the image of me just teaching and talking for the entire period, like a preacher, with the students absorbing all the knowledge that I impart to them.

Kyungso's deeply held beliefs about the "right" way to teach made it very difficult for him to explore practices that were likely to promote student learning of mathematics with understanding.

Identifying the Problem

Kyungso's lesson involved the computation of probability for compound events. In his prelesson comments, he spoke in general terms that suggested superficial knowledge of both the content and his students:

The goal in this lesson is to help the students to understand the concept of compound events, independent events, the counting principle and finally how to use the aforementioned knowledge to compute the probability of compound events. The students had reviewed some of the basics of probability during the previous lesson. In that lesson, the students reviewed the definition of outcome, sample space, and event. They also reviewed the basic rules of probability.

Based on the experience of the previous class, there is, in general, a fair level of interest among the students for the subject matter. Maybe because they were exposed to this matter in their last course, the students seem to be able to pick up on the material without too much difficulty.

Although Kyungso mentioned in his prelesson thoughts that he wanted his students to understand the material, he did not specify what they were finding difficult and how he would help them gain understanding. He suggested that students did not find the material particularly difficult. Because probability is usually a very difficult unit for students, Kyungso's comment indicates that he may not have been monitoring his students' understanding very well, if at all. Furthermore, although Kyungso mentioned several topics, he never discussed any of the details of these topics.

Kyungso's lesson plan consisted of an interesting and potentially motivational problem that required the students to take a multiple-choice quiz consisting of three questions: What is Neil Armstrong's birthday? How long is the Nile River? What is the diameter of Jupiter? The questions had 3, 4, and 2 choices, respectively, and the choices were close in value. He outlined a tight script for his lesson:

I was going to give them the quiz and then prod them to recognize the compound events by asking them if they had noticed any difference between what they did yesterday (rolling a dice and spinning the spinner) and what they are doing now. I was expecting the students to come up with the correct answer—compound events. I would then write the AIM. Following the AIM, I then planned to ask the class on what was needed to find the probability of getting all three questions correct in the quiz. I was expecting the class to reply that we needed to know the sample space. This would have provided the opening to investigate the sample spaces of this activity. The sample space investigation was to be a tree diagram to provide the necessary clarity. This was to be followed by asking the students for an easier way of getting the sample space—the counting principle. After establishing the counting principle, the plan was to then compute the probability of getting all three quiz questions correct by knowing the number of elements of the compound event or the number of ways that the compound event can take place. As a finale to the lesson, I was going to cover the counting principle with probabilities by asking the students if there is an easier way to compute the probability of the above compound event.

These prelesson thoughts reveal potentially significant problems with this lesson. Kyungso's focus was mostly on what he was going to do, with specific expectations for what the students were going to say. It was not surprising that the lesson did not proceed as Kyungso had envisioned.

The first problem he encountered was with the discourse. After the students took the quiz, one boy yelled out the correct answer to the probability question Kyungso had not yet asked (What is the probability that you will get all of the multiple choice questions correct?). Kyungso told the student that he was correct, and then he was at a loss for what to do. For the remainder of the lesson he lectured, giving the definition of a compound event and writing out a tree diagram of the sample space for the students. The students were passively taking notes, and the potential motivation of the interesting task was all but lost.

In Kyungso's postlesson conference, the supervisor raised a number of questions for discussion. Kyungso was asked to review his original goals for the lesson and see whether they were met. When he stated that he covered all of the material he planned, he was asked whether he "helped the students understand" the concepts as he stated in his original goals. He said he had tried but wasn't sure whether the students understood or not. He was asked why he didn't know, and he said. "The class was quiet. It was just my voice." He was then asked about his beliefs regarding the best ways to help students understand. Did he think it was by explaining everything to them as he had done? Through this questioning, Kyungso began to recognize that to really help students understand and be able to know if they understood, he needed to include more informative discourse in the class. He admitted that he would have to "ask more probing questions," that he would have to "hear students explain their answers," and that students would need to "respond to other students' questions." Kyungso was then asked to reconsider his knowledge regarding students. He was asked if he still thought the students did not have much difficulty with the topic, as he had stated in his prelesson thoughts. He stated again that the class was very quiet. He was asked to consider the reason for their silence. Did the fact that one student knew the answer to the unasked question at the beginning of the class mean that each of the students in the class knew the answer as well? Even if they knew the answer, did it mean that they understood why that was the answer? Perhaps it was a lucky guess? How would the teacher know if it was a lucky guess?

Kyungso was also asked to examine the nature of the task in which he engaged the students. He thought the quiz was very motivational, but the motivation ended when the student gave the probability. He was asked how he might have maintained the motivation. How could he have sustained the task so that he could develop the other concepts, such as sample space? Kyungso realized that the quietness of the class was a result of the awkward learning environment. He was asked how he might have actively engaged the students. After much questioning, Kyungso suggested that he might have recorded each of the students' answers on the test. This would have helped in developing the idea of sample space and at the same time have engaged each of the students.

Owning the Problem and Searching for Resolution

Needless to say, Kyungso was very disappointed with his lesson, but as his postlesson reflections indicated, he seemed to come to terms with many of the problematic issues of his recently enacted lesson:

> One of the major problems with my lesson was my inability to capitalize on the make-believe quiz to motivate the class to learn the subject matter. My approach was too dry and too inflexible. The class was not motivated. Some students were heard asking what was going on. I was too anxious to get the words *compound event* out of the students' mouth so I could write the AIM. Why not stir up enthusiasm by asking the class what is the probability that anyone in the class has answered all three questions correctly? Challenge the class to determine how many students answered all three questions correctly? This should lead naturally into the examination of sample space of the activity. When I did ask that question on sample space, one student answered correctly (not understanding why, however) and I applauded him for the "correct" answer and then went on to obtain the sample space by doing the tree diagram. I did all the explanation, and all the talking. Big mistake! I should have

used this opportunity to assess the students as to their understanding of sample space. Instead of applauding the student's answer, I should have asked why and how he arrived at the answer. In matter of fact, I should have addressed this question to other students to see what were they thinking of. I should have asked the students for their answers on the quiz to highlight what sample space is. Ask the students how could we determine the entire sample space. This would have been a better opportunity to ask the students to observe the difference, if any, between the type of sample space in this activity (having three outcomes) and those that involve rolling a die or spinning a spinner as they had learned in the previous lesson—as a way of introducing the concept of compound event.

In subsequent postlesson conferences, Kyungso's supervisor asked him to reexamine the impact of his teacher-centered approach on students' learning. Since he had very positive experiences in China with learning through listening, it was very difficult for him to give up his transmission approach to teaching. However, after taking a second look at various elements of his lesson: tasks, learning environment, and discourse in light of his stated goals for students, Kyungso realized that his students were not paying attention, much less learning, while he engaged in "chalk and talk." Also, through reflection and self-assessment, Kyungso came to realize that he was not monitoring student understanding sufficiently, nor was he regulating his instructional practice to fit the needs of his students.

Growth in Self-Understanding

In his final self-evaluation at the end of the semester, it appeared that Kyungso had become aware of the negative impact of his teacher-dominated approach to teaching on student learning:

> I must get rid of my old habit of tightly following the script of my lesson plan. It is a habit that I still follow in the classroom setting although I am much more aware of it now than before. In a classroom setting, I have got to learn to use the lesson plan only as a guide. I see that I am not assessing the understanding of the students continuously. Interestingly, being aware of my bad habits, I tried to observe my tutoring technique for the past few days. What I have noticed is that I do not make many of the big mistakes as I have done in the classroom setting. During tutoring, I asked a lot of questions to assess the learning level of the students, and

I tended to allow the students to learn by prodding them with questions instead of just "teach" by talking away.

Commentary

It is encouraging that Kyungso is aware of the negative impact of his beliefs about teaching mathematics on student learning with understanding. Recognition of one's problem is an important first step in the process of self-generated change. With habitual use of reflective and self-assessment strategies with respect to both his cognitions and practice, Kyungso will eventually demonstrate with consistency the kinds of classroom behaviors commensurate with student-centered professionalism.

CONCLUSION

Learning to teach is a complex process. After reading this book, you must realize that for improvement to occur, you will have to give a lot of thought to both what you do and why you do it. However, there are so many facets of teaching that unless you think about your work in a structured manner, you won't know where to start or what to do. The model we present in this book serves as a conceptual basis for the structure you can use to self-assess and reflect on your classroom teaching.

We admit that using this approach is labor intensive for both you and your college supervisor. But only a multidimensional, complex program of study can hope to adequately prepare you for a lifetime career in teaching. In our teacher education program, we have found the model to be a powerful tool for enabling teachers' growth. Perhaps the best evidence of the usefulness of the model comes from the statements made by our student teachers.

At the end of the student teaching semester, Carol wrote, "Most of the work done as a student teacher was essential for self-awareness. I think by being focused in on prelesson and postlesson thoughts, I became able to focus on them subconsciously."

Larisa said, "The fact that we had to write pre- and postlesson thoughts helped me to time and to plan my lessons better. I was also able to identify my goals for the lesson and the particular unit of work, and also to see how my ideas and beliefs had changed during the semester."

Elise acknowledged that putting into practice what you learn is very difficult: "I think that focusing on the model for teaching gave me some valuable insight into my teaching. The only problem was that I found it difficult to actually make the changes I realized were necessary after reflecting on my teaching. Maybe this should come immediately, or maybe it takes years."

Eileen had this to say about the benefits of the model:

> I would like to say that the model for teaching played an important role in my teaching development. I have learned what looks good on paper doesn't always work in a classroom. I have been able to reflect on the reasons why. Sometimes it was just a minor change. Other times there was a fundamental problem, routed deeply in a belief system. I have also been able to evaluate myself. I have seen very sound and wonderful lesson plans gone wrong due solely to my inexperience as a teacher to be able to anticipate, monitor and regulate. I realize this will come with time and have seen small improvements throughout the semester.

Teaching well is hard. Even if you have a good deal of natural talent, there is a huge amount to learn, and learning takes time. Teachers have "developmental trajectories" in which their skills evolve, moving from talented beginnings to the point where they are truly accomplished professionals (but, they *never* stop learning!). The most effective teachers—the ones whose professional growth is the fastest—are those who continually reflect on their teaching, striving to improve it. This book has provided you with the tools you can use for reflecting on your own instructional practice. We can't say it will be easy—but it will get easier as you engage in it and make reflection a habitual part of your teaching. Such reflection will ultimately be the key to your teaching expertise.

RESEARCH RESULTS
OF EXPLORATORY STUDY

Summary of Patterns
of Lesson Dimensions

Lesson Dimensions	Dimension Indicators	SC Group	M1 Group	M2 Group	TC Group
Tasks	Modes of representation	Multiple accurate representations that facilitate content clarity and enable students to connect prior knowledge and skills to the new mathematical situation.	S S S	B S	Ineffective and/or inappropriate modes of representation that impede students' efforts to build on their past mathematical understandings.
	Motivational strategies	Relevant, interesting tasks integrated throughout lesson.	B B B	B B	Tasks unrelated to student interests and/or not aligned with the goals of instruction.
	Difficulty level/sequencing	Tasks challenging yet within reach of students' abilities and sequenced so students can progress in their cumulative understanding.	S S S	B B	Tasks often too easy or too difficult for students and illogically sequenced.
Learning Environment	Social/intellectual climate	Relaxed yet businesslike atmosphere. Lesson centered on student input.	S S B	S S	Tense, awkward atmosphere. Superficial requests for and use of student input.
	Modes of instruction/pacing	Instructional strategies that support student involvement and allow time for thoughtful student input and exploration of ideas.	B B B	B T	Instructional procedures that discourage student participation and paced either too fast to involve students or too slow to maintain interest.
	Administrative routines	Effective procedures for organizing and managing the class. Students actively involved in the lesson.	S S S	S S	Administrative routines are disorderly. Students tend to be uninvolved in the work.

Lesson Dimensions	Dimension Indicators	SC Group	M1 Group	M2 Group	TC Group
Discourse	Teacher-student interactions	Teacher shows accepting attitude toward students' ideas and responds in a variety of ways to encourage students to think and reason. Students explain and justify their responses.	B B T	B T	Teacher judges student responses and resolves questions without student input. Students tend to give short responses lacking explanation or justification.
	Student-student Interaction	Students listen to and respond to each other's ideas and questions.	T T T	B B	No interaction between and among students.
	Questioning	Variety of levels and types of questions. Appropriate wait times.			Low-level, leading questions. Inappropriate wait times.

Coding method

S = Lesson dimensions resembled those of teachers in SC group.
T = Lesson dimensions resembled those of teachers in TC group.
B = Lesson dimensions resembled those of teachers in both groups.

Note. From "A Cognitive Model for Examining Teachers' Instructional Practice in Mathematics: A Guide for Facilitating Teacher Reflection," by A. F. Artzt and E. Armour-Thomas, 1999, *Educational Studies in Mathematics, 40*(3), p. 231. Copyright © 1999 by Kluwer Academic Publishers. Adapted with kind permission from Kluwer Academic Publishers.

Summary of Patterns of Cognitions

Cognitions	Components	SC group	M1 Group	M2 Group	TC group
Overarching	Knowledge of pupils	Had specific knowledge of students' prior knowledge, abilities, and attitudes.	S T S	S T	General and superficial knowledge of students.
	Knowledge of content	Viewed content in relation to entire unit and past and future study.	S S S	T T	Content viewed in isolation of past and future study.
	Knowledge of pedagogy	Anticipated specific areas of difficulty and planned suitable teaching strategies.	S S S	S T	Primary focus on time-saving management strategies to cover the content.
	Beliefs:Student's role	To think, discover, communicate, and take responsibility for learning.	T B T	S S	To stay on task.
	Beliefs: Teacher's role	To ask questions that challenge students to think for themselves and interact with one another.	T B T	S S	To model how to do problems.
	Goals	Focused primarily on conceptual understanding, procedural skills and appreciation of content.	B S B	S T	Primary focus on content coverage and students' procedural skills.
Preactive	Lesson planning:Objectives	Focused on problem-solving processes, conceptual meanings, and underlying procedures and results.	T T T	B B	Focused on procedures and results.
	Lesson planning:Structure	Sequenced problems logically from easy to more difficult. Built ideas on students' past knowledge.	S S S	B B	Sequenced problems illogically. Made large leaps in concepts and gave confusing examples.
	Lesson planning:Phases	Integrated initiation, development, and closure appropriately.	S S S	B B	Content within phases inappropriate in relation to other phases.

continued on next page

Cognitions	Components	SC group	M1 Group	M2 Group	TC group
Interactive	Monitoring	Called on students to increase participation, evaluated understanding, and adjusted instruction.	T B T	S S	Called on students to keep them on task.
	Regulation	Excluded examples to save time and added examples to increase student understanding.	T B T	T B	Made no changes from original plans.
Postactive	Evaluation	Evaluated goal accomplishment in terms of student understanding and content coverage.	T T T	S S	Evaluated goal accomplishment in terms of content coverage.
	Suggestions	Gave ideas for better monitoring of students and clearer and more interesting instructional techniques.	T T B	S S	Gave ideas for better time management.

Coding method

S = Lesson dimensions resembled those of teachers in SC group.
T = Lesson dimensions resembled those of teachers in TC group.
B = Lesson dimensions resembled those of teachers in both groups.

Note. From "A Cognitive Model for Examining Teachers' Instructional Practice in Mathematics: A Guide for Facilitating Teacher Reflection," by A. F. Artzt and E. Armour-Thomas, 1999, *Educational Studies in Mathematics, 40*(3), p. 232. Copyright © 1999 by Kluwer Academic Publishers. Adapted with kind permission from Kluwer Academic Publishers.

OBSERVATION FORMS

Observation 1:
Nature of the Content (Tasks)

Mathematics is an exciting and dynamic area of study that offers students the chance to use the power of their minds. It is essential that teachers engage students in tasks that exemplify the beauty and usefulness of mathematics. What teachers know and believe about mathematics strongly influence what they do in their classrooms and ultimately what students learn about mathematics. In addition, teachers' knowledge and beliefs about mathematics shape their goals for student learning. This observation is designed to sensitize you to the messages students are receiving about what mathematics is and what is of importance to learn. You are encouraged to use the mathematical tasks you observe as a basis for making conjectures about the cognitions of the teacher.

1. One of the widely accepted explanations of why students do not learn mathematics is the inadequacy of their teachers' knowledge of mathematics. In the lesson you observe, determine the accuracy of the mathematical content that is being taught.
   a. Record any mathematical errors, misconceptions or misrepresentations you notice.

    b. If you notice any incidences of incorrect mathematics, suggest how they should be corrected.

    c. Based on what you observe, comment on the mathematical knowledge of the teacher.

2. The NCTM standards (1989) state that one goal for students is that they learn to value mathematics. When teachers believe in and understand the value of mathematics, they can teach in a way that exposes some of the following aspects of the nature of mathematics:

- Mathematics helps us to understand our environment.
- Mathematics is the language of science.
- Mathematics is the study of patterns.
- Mathematics is a system of abstract ideas.

    a. Describe each time that the teacher explicitly pointed out the value of the mathematics they were learning. (For example, the teacher said, "This problem shows how algebra can help us to understand the world around us.")

    b. Discuss other opportunities the teacher could have used to get the students to appreciate and understand the value of the mathematics they were studying.

    c. Based on what you observed, make a conjecture regarding the teacher's goals for what the students would learn in the lesson and what these goals reflected about their beliefs about the value of the mathematical content of the lesson.

Observation 2: Discourse

Discourse is a critical aspect of the mathematics classroom and is central to the current vision of desirable mathematics teaching (NCTM 1989, 1991). The teacher's role is to create a mathematical "discourse community" (Silver & Smith, 1996). Specifically, according to the Professional Teaching Standards (NCTM, 1991) the teacher should

- Pose questions that elicit, engage, and challenge each student's thinking.
- Listen carefully to students' ideas and ask them to clarify and justify their ideas.
- Encourage students to listen to, respond to, and question the teacher and one another.

Questioning and orchestrating the discourse during a class is partly planned and also largely involves instantaneous decision making. The teacher's style of discourse is a reflection of his or her goals, knowledge, and beliefs. A good start in learning how to orchestrate discourse for maximum student understanding is to examine the discourse that takes place in other teachers' classes.

PART 1

Objective: Classroom questioning

Two of the goals for students outlined in the NCTM standards (1989) are that students learn to communicate and reason mathematically. Through effective questioning, teachers can foster such communication and reasoning.

1. Using the Questioning Skills Chart, keep a tally of the types of questions the teacher asks throughout the lesson. Record divergent questions that resemble those listed in the NCTM Professional Standards (1991, pp. 3–4).
2. In addition to categorizing the type of questions the teacher asks, keep another tally of whether the question encourages a chorus response, a volunteered response, or a teacher-selected response.
3. Using a watch that has a second hand, keep track of the time between when the teacher asks a question and when he or she receives an answer (wait time). Calculate the teacher's average wait time.
4. Based on the data you have recorded, write an overall description of the teacher's questioning style and how it affected the verbal communication that took place in the classroom. Specifically, describe how it affected the verbal participation of each of the students.
5. Give suggestions for how you feel the questioning could have been improved to maximize student understanding of the lesson.
6. Using the information you have gathered regarding the teacher's questioning of students, make conjectures regarding
   a. The teacher's knowledge of the content and knowledge of the students in this class.
   b. The teacher's beliefs about students, how they learn mathematics, and their ability to learn the mathematics being taught in this class.
   c. The teacher's goals for the students in this particular lesson.

QUESTIONING SKILLS CHART

Cognitive Level	Form of Question
Memory: Factual question	Overlaid or multiple question *Example:* Which 2 triangles are congruent and also share a common angle?
	Elliptical question *Example:* How about these two angles?
Convergent: Narrow questions	Yes-no guessing question
	Ambiguous question *Example:* How does the law of sines differ from the law of cosines?
Divergent: Broad, open-ended as suggested in the NCTM standards	Whiplash question *Example:* "The slope of this line is what?"
	Leading question *Example:* "Wouldn't you say that triangle ABC is equilateral?"
	Teacher-centered *Example:* "Give me the solution set of the equation."

Responses

Type	Number	Percent of total
Chorus		
Volunteered		
Teacher-selected		
Total		

Wait Time

QUESTIONS FROM PROFESSIONAL STANDARDS (NCTM, 1991)

1. Helping students work together to make sense of mathematics
   "What do others think about what Janine said?"
   "Do you agree? Disagree?"
   "Does anyone have the same answer but a different way to explain it?"
   "Would you ask the rest of the class that question?"
   "Do you understand what they are saying?"
   "Can you convince the rest of us that that makes sense?"

2. Helping students to rely more on themselves to determine whether something is mathematically correct
   "Why do you think that?"
   "Why is that true?"
   "How did you reach that conclusion?"
   "Does that make sense?"
   "Can you make a model to show that?"

3. Helping students learn to reason mathematically
   "Does that always work?"
   "Is that true for all cases?"
   "Can you think of a counterexample?"
   "How could you prove that?"
   "What assumptions are you making?"

4. Helping students learn to conjecture, invent, and solve problems
   "What would happen if...? What if not?"
   "Do you see a pattern?"
   "What are some possibilities here?"
   "Can you predict the next one? What about the last one?"
   "How did you think about the problem?"
   "What decision do you think he should make?"
   "What is alike and what is different about your method of solution and hers?"

5. Helping students to connect mathematics, its ideas, and its applications
   "How does this relate to...?"
   "What ideas that we have learned before were useful in solving this problem?"
   "Have we ever solved a problem like this one before?"
   "What uses of mathematics did you find in the newspaper last night?"
   "Can you give me an example of ...?"

PART 2

Classroom discourse can be observed through many different lenses. In the second class you observe, view the discourse by coding the turns that the teacher and the students take in conversing during the lesson. (See the enclosed paper, "Typical Classroom Discourse" for the definitions of the different types of turns.) Keep a tally of the turns that the teacher and the students take in the chart below.

Turns	Teacher	Student
Initiations		
Request for answer		
Request for explanation		
Responses		
State answer		
Explanations		
Reconceptualizations		
Restatements		
Expansions		
Rephrasing		
Evaluations		

After you have made the tally, create a bar graph that is a frequency distribution of teacher and student conversational contributions.

1. Write an analysis of this bar graph. What does it tell you about the discourse in the classroom, and how does it compare to what is being recommended by the NCTM standards?
2. What conjectures do you have about the teacher's beliefs about the role of the teacher and the student in the discourse that takes place in the class?
3. What suggestions do you have for changing the pattern of discourse to increase student learning?

TYPICAL CLASSROOM DISCOURSE

Turns

Initiations

Request for Answer. Speaker (teacher or student) asks another speaker (teacher or student) to provide specific declarative information without further elaboration. This category, for example, includes yes/no questions and questions about a specific computational result.

Request for Explanation. Speaker asks another speaker to elaborate on an answer previously given.

Responses

State Answer. Speaker provides information necessary for satisfying a request for an answer (specific information).

Explanations. Justifications or rationales for an answer. Explanations can be statements or a demonstration of a concept using a visual model; or a description of procedures, such as an algorithm.

Reconceptualizations

Restatements. Speaker (i.e., teacher or student) repeats verbatim what another speaker said.

Expansions. Speaker repeats what another speaker said but completes the statement by adding other necessary information.

Rephrasing. Speaker modifies previous utterance, but the meaning of the original statement is preserved.

Evaluations. Speaker makes an explicit statement about the computational accuracy, conceptual correctness, completeness, or relevance of a prior statement

Observation 3: Motivation and Teaching Strategies (Tasks, Learning Environment, Discourse)

Motivation is a key aspect of good instructional practice. Without motivation, it is difficult, if not impossible, for student learning to occur. Teachers can design lessons that maximize the chances that students' interest and curiosity will be aroused and thus be motivated to learn a particular concept. Through the use of effective teaching strategies and interesting questions, teachers can create powerful motivations for students. Of course, teachers can only accomplish this if they are convinced that it is their responsibility to do so. In addition to accepting the responsibility for motivation, teachers must have a deep knowledge of the content and related effective pedagogical strategies. They must also know their students' abilities and interests to be able to design motivational questions that will be at both an appropriate level of difficulty and be of interest to them. A first step in learning about motivation is to observe it in others' classrooms.

Observe a lesson and note the motivational and teaching strategies used.

1. Describe how the teacher tried to motivate the students to want to learn. Use the following questions as guidelines:
   a. What motivational techniques did the teacher use? What was the motivational question or questions?

     b. What teaching strategies did the teacher use to make the motivational question interesting for the students?

     c. What teaching strategies did the teacher use to maintain student motivation throughout the class period?

     d. What student behavior gave you the impression that the students were indeed motivated to learn?

2. How could the motivation for this lesson have been improved?

     a. What changes would you make to the motivational technique used by the teacher? What changes would you make to the motivational question or questions? If there were no motivational questions, what question or questions would you ask?

     b. What changes would you make to the teaching strategies that were used to create the motivation? Why do you believe this would help?

     c. What changes would you make to the teaching strategies that were used to sustain the motivation? Why do you believe this would help?

     d. What types of student behaviors would you look for to be sure that the students were motivated to learn?

3. What are your conjectures about the teacher's beliefs about motivation?

     a. How do you think this teacher would define motivation? Do you agree with this definition? Why or why not?

     b. What do you think this teacher believes his or her role is in motivating the students to learn? Why?

     c. What do you think this teacher believes the student's role is in being motivated to learn? Why?

4. What are your conjectures about the teacher's knowledge of his or her students?

     a. What did the motivational and teaching strategies reflect about the teacher's knowledge of the students' abilities?

     b. What did the motivational and teaching strategies reflect about the teacher's knowledge of the students' interests?

     c. How would you assess this teachers' knowledge of the students?

Observation 4:
Homework (Tasks, Learning Environment, Discourse, Phases, Monitoring, Regulating)

The tasks assigned to students to be completed in the privacy of their own homes play a critical role in mathematics instruction. Homework is one way of getting students actively involved in their learning of mathematics. Mathematics is not a spectator sport. Students need to practice doing many different types of problems if they are to gain proficiency and understanding of the content. When the teacher carefully selects problems, the homework can be an effective vehicle for students to find out what they do and do not understand. It is a good time for them to practice what they have learned how to do, to find out what they do not understand, and to make discoveries on their own. The problems assigned for homework should not be limited to practice of the day's lesson alone. They might include review of work from the past; work that will set the stage for future learning; work that will take time and last over the course of several days, weeks, or even months; or work that involves problem solving, research, and/or discovery.

Of course, assigning homework is only the first part of the process. The teacher has the responsibility for creating the time and means for students to discuss the work they have done on their own (discourse). The teacher also orchestrates what procedure is used (learning environment) and during what phase of the lesson it is done. Review of homework can range from having students discuss their work in small groups, to having

179

different students present their work to the class as a whole, to discussing only problems that students in the class request. Each method has its unique advantages and disadvantages and the method chosen by the teacher is usually a reflection of his or her goals for student learning, beliefs about how students learn best, and knowledge of the students.

Another part of the homework process concerns assessment (monitoring and regulating). Does the teacher check whether each student has done the homework? If so, what criteria are used? Does the teacher collect the homework? If so, does the teacher collect homework from all students or just a subset of the students? How often is homework collected? Is it checked for accuracy or for neatness? Is it graded? Are comments written on the papers or are mere check marks placed at the top? As with the procedures for reviewing homework, the different procedures used for assessing homework each have their own advantages and disadvantages, and the method chosen by the teacher is usually a reflection of his or her own overarching cognitions.

A first step in learning about the aspects of assigning, reviewing, and assessing homework is to observe the different procedures that other teachers use in their mathematics classrooms.

1. Describe the content of the homework.
   a. Discuss the apparent purpose of this particular homework assignment, (that is, review of previous day's work, motivation for new lesson, etc.)
   b. Was spiraling evident? Describe.
   c. Describe and evaluate the quality and quantity of the problems.
2. Describe the procedure used for going over the homework from the previous day.
   a. During what time period of the class was it reviewed?
   b. How long did it take?
   c. Comment on the efficiency and effectiveness of the homework review.
   d. Suggest ideas for improving the procedure used for reviewing the homework.
3. Describe the procedure used for checking the students' homework.
   a. Was individual work checked?
   b. How many students had their homework examined? When?
   c. What criteria were used for checking the work? (for example, accuracy, neatness)
   d. Comment on the efficiency and effectiveness of the homework checking.
   e. Suggest ideas for improving the procedure used for checking the homework.

4. Make conjectures regarding this teacher's underlying cognitions about homework.

   a. What do you think are the teacher's beliefs about the purpose of homework?

   b. How did the homework assignment and method of going over and checking the homework reflect the teacher's knowledge of his or her students? Of the content? Of methods of pedagogy?

5. Interview the teacher to find out more details about the homework procedures that may not have been observable to you. Use the questions below as a guide. Write your reactions to the responses of the teacher.

   a. How frequently do you assign homework?

   b. How do you create the assignment? What types of questions are assigned? How long are the assignments?

   c. What methods do you like to use to go over the homework? Do you go over all of the problems?

   d. Do you check the work that students do on their homework? If so, how? Is it graded? If so, what criteria do you use?

   e. Do you ever assign problem-solving projects, research projects, or term papers to the students? If so, please describe them.

Observation 5:
Use of Class Time
(Phases, Tasks, Learning
Environment, Discourse)

Instructional time is very precious in the secondary school setting. One of the main complaints of teachers is that they don't have enough time to work with the students. This is especially true in schools that only have periods that provide from 40 to 50 minutes of instructional time per day. It is therefore essential that teachers use their precious class time effectively and efficiently. To accomplish this, teachers must create a learning environment in which students cooperate with the teacher and one another. Furthermore teachers must create tasks that engage the students from the moment they enter the room to the moment they leave. Teachers also must orchestrate task-oriented, productive discourse. Finally, the phases of the lesson must allow for introduction, development, and closure to ideas. The way teachers make use of the limited time they have is largely an outgrowth of the priorities they have which are a reflection of their cognitions. A first step in learning about how to take maximum advantage of limited classroom time is to observe how others make use of their time.

1. Use a watch (preferably with a second hand), to record the classroom activities. Here are a couple of sample entries:

   9:00–9:05: Students enter class and open books (5 minutes)

   9:05–9:12: Teacher explains homework from previous night (7 minutes)

    a. Note where the teacher is in the room during each period of time and what he or she is doing.

    b. Note what the majority of the students are doing during each time period.

    c. Note the instructional strategies used by the teacher, such as cooperative learning, students explaining their work at the front of the board, teacher lecturing, etc.

    d. Note the phase of the lesson: initiation, development, closure.

POST-OBSERVATION FOR REPORT

2. Write the lesson plan that you believe best fits the lesson that you have observed.

3. In your lesson plan you should have identified, what you believed were, the teacher's main objectives for this particular lesson. Describe how the teacher's use of time and instructional strategies impeded or facilitated the accomplishment of the main objectives of the lesson. Give suggestions for how the use of instructional strategies and use of time could have been changed to better accomplish the goals of the lesson.

4. Describe the effect on the students, of the teacher's movement or lack of movement about the room?

5. Were all three lesson phases present in this lesson? Discuss whether their presence or absence had any discernable effect on this lesson. Give any suggestions you may have for improvement.

6. Describe how the tasks, learning environment, and discourse affected the use of class time in this lesson.

7. Based on your observations of how this teacher made use of the class time what are your conjectures regarding the teacher's knowledge, beliefs, and goals?

Observation 6:
Verbal Behavior
of Students (Discourse)

The value of having students communicate mathematically is undisputed today. The vision of an effective mathematics class is no longer one in which the teacher is talking and the students are quietly taking notes and doing problems at their seats. In the mathematics class of the 21st century students are expected to actively participate in their learning. They are expected to express themselves verbally. That is, they should be engaged in a verbal exchange of mathematical concepts with their teacher and with their classmates. It is clear that the verbal interactions that occur within a class are largely dependent on the tasks that teachers design, the learning environment they create, and the discourse they promote. Therefore, it seems reasonable to assume that teachers' cognitions (goals, knowledge, and beliefs) play a critical role in the verbal interactions that occur within a class. For example, a teacher who believes that it is essential to have all students explain their mathematical reasoning aloud and has the knowledge of instructional strategies that will engage all students in verbal mathematical communication will not just call on a select group of students, but will give all of the students a chance to participate in the discussion. It is important for you to become sensitive to the verbal interactions that occur during class so that when you teach you will be more aware of the discourse that occurs within your class.

1. Create a seating chart on a piece of blank paper. Record characteristics such as gender, socioeconomic background, ethnic or cultural differences, or any characteristics that might differentiate one individual from another.
2. Use the Legend for Verbal Flow Observations to guide you in using the appropriate arrows to record the verbal flow of the students.
3. In your analysis of the verbal flow you have observed, include responses to the following questions and any others you feel are worth considering.
   a. How many used their voice during class? Who did and who did not? What was the percentage of students who spoke?
   b. Was there an observable difference between talkers and non-talkers by gender, race, seating pattern, and/or achievement?
   c. Was there an observable difference among those who were directed to respond, those who always gave correct responses, and those who gave irrelevant responses? (Use the same descriptors as above.)
   d. Did an individual or a small group dominate? Explain.
   e. How did responses differ? Statements? Questions? etc.
   f. Was there an observable difference between those who talked about the mathematics and those who talked about non-subject matter?
4. Discuss the tasks, learning environment, and questioning style of the teacher and how you think they affected the verbal behavior you documented.
5. Make a conjecture regarding
   a. The teacher's knowledge of the students in this class.
   b. The teacher's beliefs about specific students or groups of students, how they learn mathematics, and their ability to learn the mathematics being taught in this class.
   c. The teacher's goals for the students in this particular lesson.

Legend for verbal flow observations

Symbol	Meaning of symbol

1.   Student volunteered a relevant or correct response.

2.   Student volunteered an irrelevant or incorrect response.

3.   Student volunteered a question about content.

4.   Student responded to a teacher question appropriately.

5.   Student responded to a teacher question inappropriately.

6.   Students talked to each other about the subject matter.

7.   Student talked to his or her peer about the subject matter.

8.   Student talked to his or her peer about the subject matter 4 times.

9.   Students talked to each other about non-subject matters.

10.   Student talked to his or her peer about non-subject matter.

11.   Student talked to his ore her peer about non-subject matter 3 times.

12.   Student conferred with the teacher.

186

Observation 7:
Task Orientation of Students
(Tasks, Learning
Environment, Discourse)

One of the critical concerns of beginning teachers is how to maintain discipline in their classes. The idea of losing control of adolescent students can be very frightening. Although discipline can be a great challenge in certain types of classes, the best prevention against such problems is to create well-designed tasks, a respectful learning environment, and active discourse during all phases of the lesson. A first step in learning how to do this is to observe first-hand the connection between the on-task and off-task behaviors of students and the dimensions of a lesson throughout each phase of the lesson.

For two lessons, do steps 1–5 (one lesson should be of the same class you reported on in Observation 6)

1. Construct a chart resembling the seating pattern of the class, indicating the gender, race, ethnicity, and/or any identifying characteristics of each individual.
2. Systematically examine the behavior of each student to note whether the students are on task or off task.

3. Write the letter denoting the observed behavior, "O" for on task and "F" for off task, in the box representing that student. Repeat this procedure for each student.

4. Repeat steps 2 and 3 throughout the period, after which time you will have several numbered and lettered observations noted in each box representing the various students.

5. Before Task data can be adequately analyzed, some summarizing is necessary. Construct a table with the number of students observed to be on task on the vertical axis and the times of observation on the horizontal one. Then tally the total number of each observed behavior at a given time period. For example:

	10:40	10:45	10:50	10:55
On task	17	20	25	21
Off task	13	10	5	1

6. From the chart make a line graph of the On-Task behavior. Use the number of students on the y axis and the time on the x axis.)

7. From the information in your chart answer the following questions.
   a. How many students were in this class?
   b. How many started work at the beginning of the lesson? Percentage?
   c. How long did it take before every one was at least prepared to work?
   d. At their most attentive time, how many students were working as the teacher wanted them to? Percentage?
   e. At their least attentive time, how many students were working as the teacher wanted them to? Percentage?

8. Analyze the data in terms of
   a. The variety of behaviors exhibited.
   b. The relationship between the behaviors and the different phases of the lesson.
   c. The relationship between the behaviors and the tasks, learning environment and discourse.
   d. Any other interesting relationships you notice.

9. Based on your responses to question 8, suggest ways the teacher might have improved the percentage of on-task behaviors.

10. Based on what you have observed regarding the task orientation of the students, what conjectures can you make regarding the teacher's knowledge of pedagogy and knowledge of students? What do you think are the teacher's beliefs regarding his or her role in keeping students on-task during the lesson?

11. Describe any relationships you noticed between the data you gathered from Observation 6 of this class and the data you gathered from this observation. You may state these relationships regarding individual student's behaviors or the behaviors of the class as a whole.

Observation 8: Assessment (Monitoring and Regulating)

One of the main purposes of assessment is to help teachers better understand what students know and do not know and make meaningful instructional decisions based on that information. Within our framework, this would primarily fall under the category of monitoring and regulating. Beginning teachers often think that assessment is synonymous with testing. This common misconception could not be further from the truth. Assessment is an ongoing process that takes place in classrooms every day as students and teachers interact. The fact that it is usually undocumented information should not detract from appreciating its importance. By monitoring student understanding during the class and regulating the instruction based on the feedback obtained, teachers can maximize their chances of helping students learn. In short, assessment of student understanding must be an integral part of instruction. The marks of an effective teacher are knowledge and flexibility to change the course of a lesson based on assessments of student understanding. A first step in learning how to engage in the monitoring and regulating that takes place during instruction is to observe it in other people's classrooms.

Assessment strategies are not only used to help teachers adjust their instruction. They are used as the basis for evaluation. That is, a part of every teacher's job is to assign some sort of a grade to represent the students' levels of understanding. How teachers formulate their grades is a reflection of what they value. For example, a teacher who thinks that it is important for students to be able to verbally communicate and defend their mathematical ideas will probably count class participation as part of the grade.

The purpose of this observation is to make you aware of all forms of assessment. You should be sensitive to the opportunities for assessing students during a class session and ways teachers can alter their instruction based on the information they get from students. You should also be sensitive to the many formal techniques teachers can use to assess student understanding as well as the criteria they use to evaluate students.

PART 1

Examine the questioning and responses of both teachers and students. That is, when a teacher asks a question, what is he or she trying to assess? When a student responds to the question, what assessment of student understanding can the teacher make? How does the teacher use the feedback obtained from student responses? When a student asks a question, what evaluative judgment can the teacher make? How does the teacher use that feedback to improve instruction?

1. Record any episodes of discourse that reveal how a teacher assesses during instruction, and show how the teacher used this assessment to alter the instruction. Try to include at least five examples.
2. Record any missed opportunities for making changes to the lesson based on the assessment you notice the teacher might have made. How would you have changed the lesson at that point? Justify.
3. Based on what you notice about the assessments that can be made of student understanding in this lesson and the presence or lack of regulation of the instruction, what are your conjectures regarding the teacher's knowledge and beliefs about pedagogy? Does the teacher believe it is important to monitor student understanding? If so, does the teacher know what to monitor or when to monitor? Does the teacher know how to change the course of the lesson to adapt to student needs?
4. Based on the quality of the ongoing assessment you observe, what might you say about this teacher's goals. For example, is the teacher's goal to just cover the content or do the goals incorporate student understanding? Comment.

PART 2

1. Interview each of the teachers that you observe to find out the following information:
   a. What formal methods do they use to assess student understanding (e.g., written exams, quizzes, projects, oral exams, homework, etc.)?
   b. What methods do they use to formulate grades for their students?
2. Report the results of your interviews and write your own reactions to what they have said.
3. Based on the information you have gained from the interviews, what does each teacher believe is of value for students to know, to believe. and be able to do? That is, what do you think are this teacher's goals for his or her students?

Observation 9:
Teacher Expectations
and Stereotyping
(Discourse, Tasks)

The latest recommendations of the reform movement stress the need for all students to learn mathematics—with particular emphasis on the word *all*. It is no longer acceptable for mathematical understanding to be accessible to mainly white males. Students of all races, ethnicity, socioeconomic levels, physical conditions, religions, languages, and genders must have equal opportunities to learn mathematics. Most teachers would dispute the allegation that they allow stereotyping to interfere with their ability to offer equal opportunities to all their students. But teachers' deep-rooted beliefs about the abilities of different groups of students cannot help but be reflected in their discourse with students.

For example, teachers communicate their expectations of student performance by how they respond when students have trouble with a task. Teachers who believe students are capable of carrying out tasks will suggest procedures or tell students how to do them, thus enabling the students to succeed on their own. On the other hand, teachers who believe students cannot carry out tasks will perform them for the students. When teachers do tasks for students, the students conclude that their teachers do not believe that they are capable of performing the tasks themselves. In time, students come to share the expectation of their teachers.

Another way that teachers communicate their expectations of student performance is through the length of wait time they use. There are two kinds of wait time in a classroom. The first is the time between asking a question and calling on a student, which teachers should extend to give all students an opportunity to think about an answer in preparation for being called on. We have already dealt with this type of wait time in a previous observation. The second kind is the wait time between calling on a student and achieving some kind of resolution—receiving the answer, rephrasing the question, or moving on to another student for the answer. Research shows that teachers tend to wait longer for students from whom they expect correct answers. The significance of long wait times is that they signal to students that you have confidence in their ability to answer questions, which in turn motivates students to try harder to answer them and thus to succeed.

A third way that teachers communicate their expectations of student performance is through the feedback they give to students regarding their academic performance. Although many teachers realize the instructive benefits of praising and correcting students on their written work, they are unaware and less conscious of the verbal feedback they give to students in the classroom. For example, gender studies have revealed that boys receive more feedback from teachers than girls do. Boys are both praised more for right answers and criticized more for wrong ones than girls are. One researcher even found sex-stereotyped variations on the type of feedback: Boys are encouraged to try harder when they answer a question wrong, but girls are praised for trying. When students feel that their answers receive little response from their teachers, they have less reason to work hard. These are the ones who learn less and are more likely to drop math as soon as they have the opportunity.

The purpose of this observation is to sensitize you to subtle evidences of bias in the classroom and to heighten your awareness of how beliefs about students can directly impact the nature of the discourse within the classroom.

1. Use a stop watch to record the discourse that takes place between the teacher and each student in the class by doing the following:
    a. Make a seating chart of the class indicating any observable characteristics of each of the students (e.g., gender, race/ethnicity, handicapping condition, language).

b. Use the abbreviations indicated in the following table to describe the nature of the response the teacher gives to each student.

Teacher Behavior	Symbol
Telling how or doing for	
Solves the problem for the student	T–
Carries out a task or procedure for the student	T–
Gives a student a hint for solving the problem	T+
Suggests how to carry out a task or procedure for the student to do on his or her own	T+
Wait time	
Waits less than 5 seconds	W–
Waits 5 seconds or more	W+
Giving students feedback	
Accepts a student's answer	F*
Praises a student's answer	F+
Corrects a student's answer	F–
Criticizes a student's answer	F–
Rejects a student's answer	F–

    c. Identify patterns of discourse that may have occurred with any specific groups of students.

    d. Make some conjectures regarding this teacher's beliefs about the abilities of certain groups of students. Justify your ideas.

2. Analyze the problems that are assigned to students. Are there signs of stereotyping? For example, are certain problems geared more toward the interest of males rather than females? How are people of different gender or race or ethnicity pictured in the text?

3. Analyze posters, bulletin boards, and other materials visible in the mathematics classrooms or hallways of the school. How many women and how many men are pictured? How many people of different races or ethnicity are pictured? Are any people with handicapping conditions pictured? How are they described? What are these people doing? Do any of the images or words reveal stereotypes? What do these representations suggest about the beliefs of society in general regarding the abilities of certain groups of people?

INTERACTION 1: TELLING HOW OR DOING FOR

Teacher Behavior

One way teachers communicate their expectations of student performance is how they respond when students have trouble with some task. This happens especially often in subjects that involve a lot of problem solving, such as mathematics. Teachers who believe students are capable of carrying out a given task will suggest procedures or tell students how to do it, thus enabling students to succeed on their own. Teachers who believe students cannot carry out a given task perform it for the students.

For example, research shows that teachers in mathematics and science classrooms are more likely to do academic tasks for girls than they are for boys. They are more likely to tell girls the theorem needed to complete the proof but to ask boys to think about what theorem is needed. They are more likely to prepare the microscope slide for girls but to tell boys how to prepare the slide. Students who are "done for" draw the conclusion that the teacher believes they are not capable of performing the task, and in time, students come to share the expectations of the teacher.

Coding Method

– = Solve a problem for a student.
– = Carry out a task or procedure for a student.
+ = Give a student a hint for solving a problem.
+ = Suggest how a student can carry out a task or procedure on her or his own.

INTERACTION 2: WAIT TIME

Teacher Behavior

There are two kinds of wait times in a classroom. The first is the time between asking a question and calling on a student, which teachers should extend to give all students an opportunity to think about an answer in preparation for being called on.

The second kind is the wait time between calling on a student and achieving some kind of resolution—receiving the answer, rephrasing the question, or moving on to another student for the answer. Research shows that teachers tend to wait longer for students from whom they expect correct answers. They tend to wait longer for interpretative and opinion answers than for fact answers. They tend to wait longer for answers from boys in math and science classes, and longer for answers from girls in English classes.

The significance of long wait time, then, is that it signals to students that you have confidence in their ability to answer questions, which in turn motivates students to try harder and thus to succeed.

Coding Method

– = Wait time of less than 5 seconds.
+ = Wait time of 5 seconds or more.

INTERACTION 3: GIVING STUDENTS FEEDBACK

Teacher Behavior

Feedback to students' academic performance can be almost as important to their learning as the original lesson. Teachers usually know how instructive praising and correcting can be and therefore take a great deal of care with students' written work. Verbal feedback in the classroom is just as important as written feedback but is usually much less conscious.

Gender studies have revealed that boys receive more feedback from teachers than girls do. Boys are both praised more for right answers and criticized more for wrong ones than girls are. One researcher even found sex-stereotyped variations on the type of feedback: boys are encouraged to try harder when they answer a question wrong but girls are praised for trying.

If students feel that their answers receive little response from their teachers, they have less reason to work hard. These are the ones who learn less and are more likely to drop math as soon as they have the opportunity.

Coding Method

0 = Accept a student's answer
+ = Praise a student's answer
– = Correct a student's answer
– = Criticize a student's answer
– = Reject a student's answer

Observation 10:
Culminating Activity

In the previous nine observation assignments, you were asked to note different aspects of teachers' instructional practice and to make conjectures for the underlying teacher cognitions that could account for what you observed. Specifically, you were asked to critique the tasks, learning environment, and discourse, as well as the teacher's use of phases and monitoring and regulating of instruction. Based on this information, you were asked to consider what the teachers' knowledge, beliefs, and goals were. In this observation, you put all you have learned together by observing and critiquing all aspects of instruction in one lesson and making conjectures regarding all aspects of the teacher's cognition.

This report will not be done as a written essay but will be organized in the form of a list. You will use the categories given below to organize your presentation of ideas.

ASSESSING INSTRUCTIONAL PRACTICE

Use the three broad categories you have focused on all semester (tasks, learning environment, discourse) to assess the instructional practice of the teacher. In addition to focusing on all of the variables outlined in your previous observations, use the nine subcategories shown in the following outline to organize your discussion.

TASKS

1. Modes of representation. Give a description of the symbols, materials, etc., the teacher used, and evaluate their effectiveness in facilitating content clarity and enabling students to connect their prior knowledge and skills to the new mathematical situation.
2. Motivational strategies. Describe the strategies used to capture students' curiosity, and assess whether or not they inspired students to speculate and pursue conjectures about the mathematical concepts. Discuss whether the diversity of student interests was taken into account and if the substance of the motivation was aligned with the goals and purposes of instruction.
3. Sequencing and difficulty levels. Describe how the tasks were sequenced and the difficulty level of the tasks, and evaluate whether they enabled the students to progress in their cumulative understanding of the content area. Also discuss whether the sequencing facilitated the students' ability to make connections between the ideas they learned in the past and those they were expected to learn in this lesson.

LEARNING ENVIRONMENT

4. Social and intellectual climate. Assess to what degree the teacher established and maintained a positive rapport with and among students by showing respect for and valuing students' ideas and ways of thinking. Also, discuss whether the teacher enforced classroom rules and procedures so that the students behaved appropriately.
5. Modes of instruction and pacing. Describe the instructional strategies used. Assess how they encouraged and supported student involvement and at the same time supported the attainment of the goals for the lesson. Also, discuss whether the teacher provided and structured the time neces-

sary for the students to express themselves and explore mathematical ideas and problems.

6. Administrative routines. Describe and assess the procedures used for organization and management of the classroom.

DISCOURSE

7. Teacher-student interaction. Assess whether the teacher communicated with students in a nonjudgmental manner and encouraged the participation of each student. Describe whether the teacher required students to give full explanations and justifications or demonstrations orally and/or in writing. Also, determine whether the teacher listened carefully to students' ideas and made appropriate decisions regarding when to offer information, provide clarification, model, lead and let students grapple with difficulties.

8. Student-student interaction. Describe whether and how the teacher encouraged students to listen to, respond to, and question each other so that they could evaluate and, if necessary, discard or revise ideas and take full responsibility for arriving at mathematical conjectures and/or conclusions.

9. Questioning. Assess the questioning style of the teacher and determine whether she or he posed a variety of levels and types of questions using appropriate wait times that elicited, engaged, and challenged students' thinking.

ASSESSING TEACHER COGNITIONS

Use the categories you have focused on all semester to make conjectures regarding the teacher's cognitions. In addition to focusing on all of the cognitions outlined in your previous observations, use the categories outlined below to organize your discussion.

Preactive: Overarching Cognitions

1. Goals. Describe what you think the teacher's goals were for this lesson. Assess to what degree she or he wanted to help students construct their own meaning so that they would develop conceptual as well as procedural understanding and would value the mathematics and feel confident in their abilities.

2. Knowledge of pupils. Assess to what degree the teacher knew the students' prior knowledge, experiences, abilities, attitudes, and interests.
3. Knowledge of content. Assess to what degree the teacher had conceptual and procedural understanding of the content and whether or not she or he viewed the content in relation to the entire unit and past and future study.
4. Knowledge of pedagogy. Assess the teacher's understanding of how students learn mathematics and whether or not she or he anticipated specific areas of difficulty and planned suitable teaching.
5. Beliefs about the student's role. Assess how the teacher viewed the students' role in the classroom. To what degree did she or he view students as active participants in the lesson who must think, reason, discover, communicate, and take responsibility for learning.
6. Beliefs about the content. Assess what you believe are the teacher's beliefs about the mathematical content. To what degree did she or he view mathematics as an exciting and worthwhile area of study that is a "dynamic and expanding system of principles and ideas constructed through exploration and investigation" (NCTM, 1991, p.133).
7. Beliefs about the role of the teacher. Assess how the teacher viewed his or her role in the classroom. To what degree did she or he view her- or himself as a facilitator of student learning by selecting tasks and asking questions that challenge students to think for themselves and interact with one another?

Interactive Cognitions

8. Monitoring. Assess the thoughts you think the teacher had during the course of instruction. For example, to what degree did the teacher observe, listen to, elicit participation of students to increase participation and assess student learning and disposition toward mathematics for the purpose of adjusting instruction.
9. Regulating. Assess to what degree you believe the teacher adapted instruction while teaching based on the information she or he received through monitoring student learning and interest.

Postactive Cognitions

If possible, interview the teacher at the conclusion of the lesson to obtain his or her evaluation of the lesson and how he or she might improve it if he or she were to teach it again. If you complete this interview, you can then evaluate the teacher's postactive cognitions.

10. Self-assessing. When the teacher spoke about the lesson, to what degree did she or he assess goal accomplishment in terms of student understanding, and to what degree was it assessed in terms of content coverage?

11. Reflecting. After the lesson, did the teacher give any suggestions for ways to improve the lesson? What was the nature of each suggestion? For example, did the teacher suggest ways to better monitor students and use clearer and more interesting instructional techniques?

OBSERVATION CHARTS MADE BY PRESERVICE TEACHERS

Verbal Interaction Chart

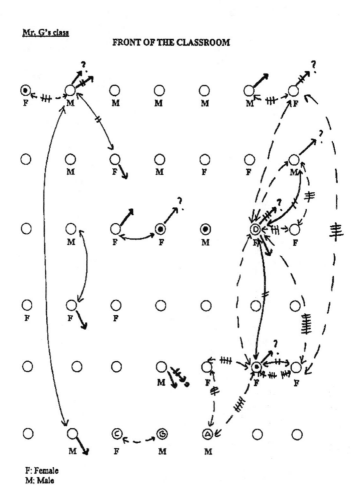

Line Graph of At-Task Behaviors

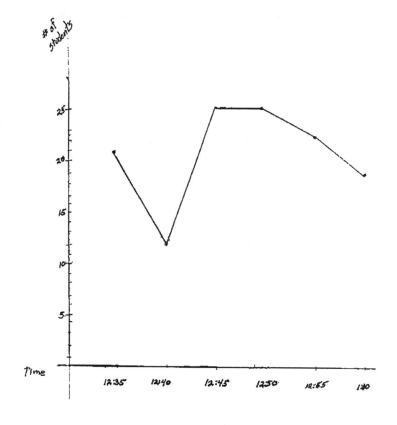

	12:35	12:40	12:45	12:50	12:55	1:00
AT TASK	21	12	25	25	22	18
OFF Task	4	13	0	0	3	7

Chart and Line Graph of At-Task Behaviors

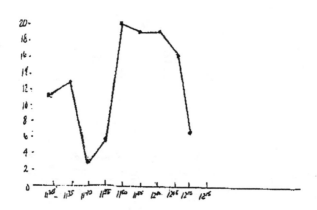

GUIDES AND FORMS FOR SUPERVISED OBSERVATIONS

Guide for Observation Written Reports and Conference

You should consider your observation day as an opportunity to get feedback on your teaching, share ideas, and learn more about yourself as a mathematics teacher. To ensure that you will maximize your learning, follow these guidelines.

1. Before you start your lesson, submit a copy of your lesson plan and your prelesson thoughts to the supervisor. (Use the directions in Appendix D-2.)
2. After the lesson, share your ideas about the lesson.
   a. Describe your general thoughts about the lesson. Use the following questions as a structure for your comments.
      i. What were your original goals for this lesson?
      ii. How did you plan on accomplishing these goals?
      iii. Do you think you accomplished your goals?
      iv. How did your plan compare with what you actually did?
      v. Explain some of the decisions you made that accounted for the differences.
   b. Give detailed explanations of what occurred during the lesson, the decisions you made while teaching, and your assessment of what you did. To be sure that you address all aspects of your instructional practice, consult Table 1 and address the following questions:

i. Examine the list of suggested ideas for tasks. In terms of the given categories, assess the tasks in which you engaged your students. Discuss the strengths and weaknesses of these tasks. How might you improve it?

ii. Examine the categories for learning environment. In terms of these categories, assess the learning environment you created in your class. Suggest ways you might improve it.

iii. Examine the list of suggested ways to conduct discourse. Compare your behaviors with those recommended on the list. What accounts for any differences you detect? How might you improve the discourse?

3. The supervisor and cooperating teacher discuss what you have said and their ideas about the lesson.

After you have completed your lesson analysis, the cooperating teacher and the supervisor share their ideas about the lesson, request clarification of issues, and help you think about what new knowledge you have gained or beliefs you may have changed as a result of teaching the lesson. They might also give suggestions for additional ways to improve the lesson. During this conference, it is important that you do the following:

a. Be sure to take notes so that you will have an accurate and detailed account of the complete discussion.

b. Remember that this is a professional conference about teaching mathematics. To maximize your learning, try to be open-minded about what is discussed, not to take suggestions or criticisms personally, and above all, not to be defensive. On the other hand, be sure that you express any ideas you have, ask questions, and debate interesting issues in a professional manner.

4. Reflect on and assess the lesson again in your written postlesson activity.

Now that you have engaged in your own reflection and assessment of the lesson with the help of your supervisor and cooperating teacher, it is important that you revisit all the ideas that each of you came up with and discussed. In addition to writing your postlesson thoughts, use the forms listed below to assess the instructional practice of your lesson. (Submit all written documents at the next seminar.)

a. Written Postlesson Thoughts and Assessment (Appendix D-3)

b. Self-Assessment of Instructional Practice (Appendix D-4)

c. Summary of Self-Assessment (Appendix D-5)

Written Observation Report
Before the Lesson

All observations by supervisors are scheduled in advance. When the supervisor arrives at your school, you must hand him or her your prelesson thoughts and your lesson plan.

PRELESSON THOUGHTS

The purpose of the prelesson thoughts is twofold. First, it gives the supervisor the background information needed to better understand your reasons for creating and conducting the lesson as you did. Second, it heightens your awareness of the issues you should attend to when creating a lesson.

Follow these steps to write your prelesson thoughts:

1. Provide any personal background information that you think is important for the supervisor to be aware of (for example, conflicts with the cooperating teacher, dilemmas you face, etc.).
2. Describe your goals for students.
3. Describe the knowledge you have of these students (such as ability levels, interests) and how you will use that knowledge to shape your lesson.

4. Describe the knowledge you have of the content (for example, its place in the curriculum, its importance) and how you will use that knowledge to shape your lesson.
5. Describe the knowledge you have of different pedagogical strategies you can use for this lesson and why you are choosing one approach rather than another.
6. Describe the sources you are using to get ideas for this lesson.
7. Describe any difficulties that you are anticipating and how you intend on dealing with them should they arise.

LESSON PLAN

Objectives

State the aim of the lesson and clearly describe your performance and understanding objectives for the students.

Structure

Clearly identify the motivation for the lesson. Sequence the tasks logically, building on previous student understanding and using appropriate instructional strategies so you address the needs of all students. Identify how you will actively involve students in constructing ideas.

Phases

Indicate the phases for each segment of the lesson: (1) initiation (establishing students' readiness for learning); (2) development (building new concepts) and; (3) closure (integrating and extending new concepts).

Written Observation Report After the Lesson

POSTLESSON THOUGHTS AND ASSESSMENT

Some of the most important learning comes from reflections about lessons already taught. It is important to use both good and bad experiences to your advantage. Write a report about what you learned from your teaching experience and the postlesson conference. Try to address each of the following topics as well as any other issues that you would like to discuss.

1. Goals
   Consider your original goals for the lesson. Did you accomplish these goals?
   How do you know?
2. Knowledge
   Describe what new ideas you may have learned about the content, the students, or the best ways of teaching the lesson.
3. Beliefs
   Describe what beliefs you had about the content, the students, or the best ways of teaching the lesson that changed in some way.
4. Monitoring and Regulating
   Describe some of the thoughts you had during the lesson that caused you to make the decisions you made.

5. Evaluating and Suggesting
   a. How well do you feel you evaluated the lesson at the postlesson conference?
   b. What points are you aware of now that you weren't aware of then, if any?
   c. What do you feel were the strong points of the lesson?
   d. What do you feel were the weak points of the lesson?
   e. If you were to teach this lesson again, what would you do differently? Why?
   f. If you feel it is necessary, submit a revised lesson plan.

Self-Assessment
of Instructional Practice

Name_____

Indicators Evaluation

	N/O	1	2	3
Tasks				
Modes of representation				
Motivational strategies				
Sequencing and difficulty levels				
Learning environment				
Social and intellectual climate				
Modes of instruction and pacing				
Administrative routines				
Discourse				
Teacher-student interactions				
Student-student interactions				
Questioning				

Evaluation Scale

See Table 1 for a description of the indicators.
3 = Commendable; strong presence of indicator.
2 = Satisfactory; indicator is somewhat present.
1 = Needs attention; no presence of indicator.
N/O = Not observed or not applicable.

Include an explanation of your ratings in your postlesson thoughts and assessment.

Summary
Self-Assessment Form

Name:_____   School:_____
Observation no. _____   Cooperating teacher: _____
Grade: _____   Class/group ability: _____
Lesson:_____
Date:_____

Strong points of lesson:

1. _____
    _____
2. _____
    _____
3. _____
    _____

Areas for improvement:

1. _____
    _____
2. _____
    _____
3. _____
    _____

Student's signature:_____

Supervisor's signature: _____

Evaluation of Teacher Cognitions

INDICATORS	EVALUATIONS				COMMENTS
	N/O	1	2	3	
I. PREACTIVE					
A) Goals					
B) Knowledge					
1. Pupils					
2. Content					
3. Pedagogy					
C) Lesson Plan					
1. Objectives					
2. Structure					
3. Phases					
II. CONFERENCE ANALYSIS					
III. POSTACTIVE					
A) Written Evaluation of Lesson After the Conference					
B) Suggestions for Revision					

Evaluation Scale

See Table 2 for a listing of the indicators.
3 = Commendable; strong presence of the indicator
2 = Satisfactory; moderate presence of the indicator
1 = Needs attention; no presence of the indicator
N/O = Not observed or not applicable.

Videotaped Lesson—Final Conference

Before the end of the semester, make a final videotape of a lesson that you teach as part of your student teaching requirements. Use this tape to

- Demonstrate your ability to reflect on and assess your own lesson as well as your own cognitions.
- Identify aspects of the tape that you can share with your supervisor that will exemplify what you have described in your written documents.
- Document areas in which you have changed, based on previous videotapes. The specific directions are listed below.

PART 1

Self-Assessment of Videotaped Lesson

1. Write your prelesson thoughts for the lesson you plan to videotape (see Appendix D-2).
2. Write your lesson plan.
3. Videotape your lesson.
4. After you view the videotape of your lesson, complete the form for the self-assessment of your instructional practice, write your postlesson thoughts

and assessment, and complete the Self-Assessment Forms (see Appendixes D-4 and D-5).

5. Evaluate your own cognitions by filling out the form that your supervisor usually completes: Evaluation of Teacher Cognitions (See Appendix D-6).

PART 2

Reviewing Videotape With Your Supervisor

6. To prepare for the conference with your supervisor, locate specific points in your videotape that illustrate the most important of your postlesson thoughts. Remember, both strong points and weak points are equally important to point out. Decision-making points are essential to identify. The more organized you are, the better the conference will be. Write the number or section of the tape of each teaching episode, and write your comments beside that number.

PART 3

Assessing Your Professional Growth by Comparing Past and Present Videotapes

7. Select an aspect of your teaching that you believe improved over the course of the semester and that you can document by showing "before and after" video examples. Write a few paragraphs that discuss what you believe contributed to your improvement. For example, discuss how any of your beliefs or knowledge might have changed and what caused them to change.

References

Armour-Thomas, E., & Szczesiul, E. (1989). *A review of the knowledge base of the Connecticut Competency Instrument.* Hartford: Connecticut State Department of Education, Bureau of Research and Teacher Assessment.

Artzt, A. F. (1999). A structure to enable preservice teachers of mathematics to reflect on their teaching. *Journal of Mathematics Teacher Education, 2,* 143–166.

Artzt, A. F., & Armour-Thomas, E. (1992). Development of a cognitive-metacognitive framework for protocol analysis of mathematical problem solving in small groups. *Cognition and Instruction, 9,* 137–175.

Artzt, A. F., & Armour-Thomas, E. (1998). Mathematics teaching as problem solving: A framework for studying teacher metacognition underlying instructional practice in mathematics. *Instructional Science, 26,* 5–25.

Artzt, A. F., & Armour-Thomas, E. (1999). A cognitive model for examining teachers' instructional practice in mathematics: A guide for facilitating teacher reflection. *Educational Studies in Mathematics, 40*(3), 211–235.

Artzt, A.F., & Armour-Thomas E. (2001). Mathematics teaching as problem solving: A framework for studying teacher metacognition underlying instructional practice in mathematics. In H. Hartman (Ed.), *Metacogniton in learning and instruction: Theory, research and practice* (pp. 127–148) Dordrecht, The Netherlands: Kluwer.

Ball, D. L. (1990). Prospective elementary and secondary teachers' understanding of division. *Journal for Research in Mathematics Education, 21,* 132–144.

Bartlett, F.C. (1932). *Remembering.* Cambridge: Cambridge University Press.

Borko, H., & Livingston, C. (1989). Cognition and improvisation: Differences in mathematics instruction by expert and novice teachers. *American Educational Research Journal, 26*(4), 473–498.

Borko, H., & Putnam, R. (1996). Learning to teach. In D. C. Berliner & R. C. Calfee (Eds.), *Handbook of educational psychology* (pp. 673–708). New York: Macmillan.

Bossert, S. (1977). Tasks, group management, and teacher control behavior: A study of classroom organization and teacher style. *School Review, 85,* 552–565.

Brown, A. L. (1978). Knowing when, where, and how to remember: A problem of metacognition. In R. Glaser (Ed.), *Advances in instructional psychology* (Vol. 1, pp. 77–165). Hillsdale, NJ: Lawrence Erlbaum Associates.

Brown, C.A., & Baird, J. (1993). Inside the teacher: Knowledge, beliefs, and attitudes. In P.S. Wilson (Ed.), *Research ideas for the classroom: High school mathematics* (pp. 245–259). New York,: Macmillan.

Brown, C. A., & Borko, H. (1992). Becoming a mathematics teacher. In D. A. Grouws (Ed.), *Handbook of research on mathematics teaching and learning* (pp. 209–239). New York: Macmillan.

Brown, J. S., Collins, A., & Duguid, P. (1989). Situated cognitions and the culture of learning. *Educational Researcher, 18*(1), 32–42.

Campbell, P. G. (1995). Redefining the "Girl Problem in Mathematics." In W. G. Secada, E. Fennema, & L. Adajian (Eds.), *New directions for equity in mathematics education* (pp. 225–41). New York: Cambridge Univeristy Press.

Cazden, C. B. (1986). Classroom discourse. In M. C. Wittrock (Ed.), *Handbook of research on teaching* (pp. 432–463). New York: Macmillan.

Chi, M. (1978). Knowledge structures and memory development. In R. Siegler (Ed.), *Children's thinking: What develops?* (pp. 73–96). Hillsdale, NJ: Lawrence Erlbaum Associates.

Clark, C. M., & Peterson, P. L. (1986). Teachers' thought processes. In M. C. Wittrock (Ed.), *Handbook of research on teaching* (3rd ed., pp. 255–296). New York: Macmillan.

Cobb, P. (1986). Contexts, goals, beliefs, and learning mathematics. *For the Learning of Mathematics, 6*(2), 2–9.

Cohen, D. (1990). A revolution in one classroom: The case of Mrs. Oublier. *Education Evaluation and Policy Analysis, 12*(3), 311–329.

Confrey, J. (1990). What constructivism implies for teaching. In R. Davis, C. Maher, & N. Noddings (Eds.), *Constructivist views on the teaching and learning of mathematics* (pp. 107–122). Reston, VA: NCTM.

Cooney, T. P. (1985). A beginning teacher's view of problem solving. *Journal for Research in Mathematics Education, 16*(5), 324–336.

Cooney, T. J. (1993). On the notion of authority applied to teacher education. In J. R. Becker & B. J. Pence (Eds.), *Proceedings of the fifteenth annual meeting of the North American chapter of the International Group for the Psychology of Mathematics Education* (Vol. 1, pp. 40–46). San Jose, CA: San Jose State University.

Cooney, T. J., & Shealy, B. (1997). On understanding the structure of teachers' beliefs and their relationship to change. In E. Fennema & B. S. Nelson (Eds.), *Mathematics teachers in transition* (pp. 87–110). Mahwah, NJ: Lawrence Erlbaum Associates.

Cooney, T. J., Shealy, B., & Arvold, B. (1998). Conceputalizing belief structures of preservice secondary mathematics teachers. *Journal for Research in Mathematics Education, 29,* 306–333.

Dewey, J. (1933). *How we think: A restatement of the relation of reflective thinking to the educative process.* Boston: D.C. Heath.

Ernest, P. (1989). The knowledge, beliefs and attitudes of the mathematics teacher: A model. *Journal of Education for Teaching, 15(1),* 13–33.

Fennema, E., Carpenter, T. P., Franke, M .L., Levi, L., Jacobs, V. R., & Empson, S. B. (1996). A longitudinal study of learning to use children's thinking in mathematics instruction. *Journal for Research in Mathematics Education, 27,* 403–434.

Fennema, E., Carpenter, T. P., & Peterson, P. L. (1989). Teachers' decision making and cognitively guided instruction: A new paradigm for curriculum development. In N. F. Ellerton & M. A. Clements (Eds.), *School mathematics: The challenge to change* (pp. 174–187). Geelong, Victoria, Australia: Deakin University Press.

Fennema, E., & Franke, M. L. (1992). Teachers' knowledge and its impact. In D. Grouws (Ed.), *Handbook of research on mathematics teaching and learning* (pp. 147–164). New York: Macmillan.

Flavell, J. H. (1981). Cognitive monitoring. In W. P. Dickson (Ed.), *Children's oral communication skills* (pp. 35–60). New York: Academic Press.

Franke, M., Fennema, E., & Carpenter, T. P. (1997). Changing teachers: Interactions between beliefs and classroom practice. In E. Fennema & B. S. Nelson (Eds.), *Mathematics teachers in transition* (pp. 255–282). Mahwah, NJ: Lawrence Erlbaum Associates.

Garofalo, J., & Lester, F. K. (1985). Metacognition, cognitive monitoring, and mathematical performance. *Journal for Research in Mathematics Education, 16,* 163–176.

Goldsmith, L., & Schifter, D. (1997). Understanding teachers in transition: Characteristics of a model for developing teachers. In E. Fennema & B. S. Nelson (Eds.), *Mathematics teachers in transition* (pp. 19–54). Mahwah, NJ: Lawrence Erlbaum Associates.

Good, T. L., & Brophy, J. (1995). *Contemporary educational psychology.* New York: Longman.

Greeno, J. G. (1989). A perspective on thinking. *American Psychologist, 44,* 134–141.

Harris, K. R. (1979). Developing self-regulated learners: The role of private speech and self-instructions. *Educational Psychologist, 25*(1), 35–49.

Hiebert, J., (Ed.). (1986). *Conceptual knowledge and procedural knowledge: The case of mathematics.* Hillsdale, NJ: Lawrence Erlbaum Associates.

Hiebert, J., & Carpenter, T. P. (1992). Learning and teaching with understanding. In D. Grouws (Ed.), *Handbook of research on mathematics teaching and learning* (pp. 65–97). New York: Macmillan.

Hill, J., Yinger, R. J., & Robbins, D. (1981, April). *Instructional planning in a developmental preschool.* Paper presented at the annual meeting of the American Educational Research Association, Los Angeles.

Hinsley, D. A., Hayes, J. R., & Simon, H. A. (1977). From words to equation: Meaning and representation in algebra word problems. In M. A. Just & P. A. Carpenter (Eds.), *Cognitive processes in comprehension* (pp. 89–106). Hillsdale, NJ: Lawrence Erlbaum Associates.

Jackson, P. W. (1968). *Life in classrooms.* New York: Holt, Rinehart & Winston.

Jaworski, B. (1994). *Investigating mathematics teaching: A constructivist enquiry.* London: Falmer Press.

Jones, B. F., Palincsar, A. S., Ogle, D. S., & Carr, E. G. (1987). Strategic teaching: A cognitive focus. In B. F. Jones, A. S. Palincsar, D. S. Ogle, & E. G. Carr (Eds.), *Strategic teaching and learning: Cognitive instruction in the content areas* (pp. 33–63). Alexandria, VA: ASCD.

Kemmis, S. (1985). Action research and the politics of reflection. In D. Boud, R. Keogh, & D. Walker (Eds.), *Reflection: Turning experience into learning.* London: Kogan Page.

Klinzing, G., Klinzing-Eurich, G., & Tisher, R. (1985). Higher cognitive behaviors in classroom discourse: Congruencies between questions and pupils' responses. *Australian Journal of Education, 29,* 63–75.

Kounin, J., & Gump, P. (1974). Signal systems of lesson settings and the task-related behavior of pre-school children. *Journal of Educational Psychology, 66,* 554–562.

Lampert, M. L. (1985). How teachers teach. *Harvard Educational Review, 55*, 229–246.

Lampert, M. L. (1986). Knowing, doing, and teaching multiplication. *Cognition and Instruction, 3*, 305–342.

Leinhardt, G., & Greeno, J. G. (1986). The cognitive skill of teaching. *Journal of Educational Psychology, 78*, 75–95.

Leiva, M. A. (1995). Empowering teachers through the evaluation process. *Mathematics Teacher, 88*(1), 44–47.

Livingston, C., & Borko, H. (1990). High school mathematics review lessons: Expert-novice distinction. *Journal for Research in Mathematics Education, 21*, 372–387.

Mathematical Sciences Education Board (MSEB) and National Research Council (NRC). (1991). *Counting on you: Actions supporting mathematics teaching standards.* Washington, DC: National Academy Press.

National Council of Teachers of Mathematics. (1989). *Curriculum and evaluation standards for school mathematics.* Reston, VA: NCTM.

National Council of Teachers of Mathematics. (1991). *Professional standards for teaching mathematics.* Reston, VA: The Council.

National Council of Teachers of Mathematics. (2000). *Principles and standards for school mathematics.* Reston, VA: NCTM.

Newell, A. (1980). Physical symbol systems. *Cognitive Science, 4*, 135–183.

Noddings, N. (1990). Constructivism in mathematics education. In R. Davis, C. Maher, & N. Noddings (Eds.), *Constructivist views on the teaching and learning of mathematics: Journal for Research in Mathematics Education: Monograph Number 4.* Reston, VA: NCTM.

Oakes, J. (1990). Opportunities, achievement, and choice: Women and minority students in science and mathematics. *Review of Research in Education, 16*, 153–222.

Pajares, F. (1992). Teachers beliefs and educational research: Cleaning up a messy concept. *Review of Educational Research, 62*, 307–332.

Paris, S. G., & Newman, R. S. (1990). Developing aspects of self-regulated learning. *Educational Psychologist, 25*(1), 87–102.

Perkins, D. N., & Salomon, G. (1989). Are cognitive skills context bound? *Educational Researcher, 18*(1), 16–25.

Peterson, P. L. (1988). Teachers' and students' cognitional knowledge for classroom teaching and learning. *Educational Researcher, 17*(5), 5–14.

Peterson, P. L., Fennema, E., Carpenter, T. P., & Loef, M. (1989). Teachers' pedagogical content beliefs in mathematics. *Cognition and Instruction, 6*, 1–40.

Peterson, P. L., Marx, R. W., & Clark, C. M. (1978). Teacher planning, teacher behavior, and student achievement. *American Educational Research Journal, 15*, 417–432.

Polya, G. (1945). *How to solve it.* Garden City, NJ: Doubleday.

Posamentier, A.S., & Stepelman, J. (1999). *Teaching secondary school mathematics: techniques and enrichment units (5th edition).* Upper Saddle River, NJ: Merrill.

Richards, J. (1991). Mathematical discussions. In E. Von Glasersfeld (Ed.), *Radical constructivism in mathematics education* (pp. 13–51). Dordrecht, The Netherlands: Kluwer.

Rogers, C. (1983). *Freedom to learn: For the 80's.* Columbus, OH: Merrill.

Rogoff, B., & Lave, J. (1984). *Everyday cognition: its development in social context.* Cambridge, MA: Harvard University Press.

Rowe, M. (1974). Wait-time and rewards as instructional variables. *Journal of Research in Science Teaching, 11,* 81–94.

Rowe, M. (1986). Wait time: Slowing down may be a way of speeding up! *Journal of Teacher Education, 37,* 43–50.

Rumelhart, D. E. (1975). Notes on a schema for stories. In D. B. Bobrow & A. M. Collins (Eds.). *Representation and understanding* (pp. 211–236). New York: Academic Press.

Samson, G., Strykowski, B., Weinstein, T., & Walberg, H. (1987). The effects of teacher questioning levels on student achievement: A quantitative synthesis. *Journal of Educational Research, 80,* 290–295.

Saphier, J., & Gower, R. (1987). *The skillful teacher: Building your teaching skills.* MA: Better Teaching, Inc.

Schifter, D., & Simon, M. A. (1992). Assessing teachers' development of a constructivist view of mathematics learning. *Teaching and Teacher Education 8(2),* 187–197.

Schoenfeld, A. H. (1987). What's all the fuss about metacognition? In A. H. Schoenfeld (Ed.), *Cognitive science and mathematics education* (pp. 189–215). Hillsdale, NJ: Lawrence Erlbaum Associates.

Schoenfeld, A. H. (1998). Toward a theory of teaching-in-context. *Issues in Education, 4(1),* 1–94.

Schon, D. A. (1983). *The reflective practitioner: How professionals think in action.* New York: Basic Books.

Schram, P., Wilcox, S., Lappan, G., & Lanier, P. (1989). Changing preservice beliefs about mathematics education. In C.A. Maher, G. A. Goldin, & R. B. Davis (Eds.), *Proceedings of the eleventh annual meeting of the North American chapter of the International Group for the Psychology of Mathematics Education* (pp. 296–302). New Brunswick, NJ: Rutgers University, Center for Mathematics, Science and Computer Education.

Secada, W. G. (1992). Race, ethnicity, social class, language, and achievement in mathematics. In D. Grouws (Ed.), *Handbook of research and mathematics teaching and learning* (pp. 623–60). New York: Macmillan Publishing Co.

Shavelson, R. J., & Stern, P. (1981). Research on teachers' pedagogical thoughts, judgments, decisions and beliefs. *Review of Educational Research, 51,* 455–498.

Shulman, L. S. (1986). Those who understand: Knowledge growth in teaching. *Educational Researcher, 15,* 4–14.

Silver, E. A. (1985). Research on teaching mathematical problem solving: Some underrepresented themes and needed directions. In E. A. Silver (Ed.), *Teaching and learning mathematical problem solving: Multiple research perspectives* (pp. 247–266). Hillsdale, NJ: Lawrence Erlbaum Associates.

Silver, E. A. (1986). Using conceptual and procedural knowledge: A focus on relationships. In J. Hiebert (Ed.), *Conceptual and procedural knowledge: The case of mathematics* (pp. 181–198). Hillsdale, NJ: Lawrence Erlbaum Associates.

Silver, E. A., & Smith M. S. (1996). Building discourse communities in mathematics classrooms. In P. C. Elliot (Ed.), 1996 Yearbook: *Communication in mathematics K–12 and beyond* (pp. 20–28). Reston, VA: National Council of Teachers of Mathematics.

Simon, M. A. (1997). Developing new models of mathematics teaching: An imperative for research on mathematics teacher development. In E. Fennema & B. S. Nelson (Eds.), *Mathematics in transition* (pp. 55–86). Mahwah, NJ: Lawrence Erlbaum Associates.

Sternberg, R. J. (1986). *Intelligence applied: Understanding and increasing your intellectual skills.* New York: Harcourt, Brace, Jovanovich.

Swafford, J. O. (1995). Teacher preparation. In I. M. Carl (Ed.), *Prospects for school mathematics* (pp. 157–174). Reston, VA: NCTM.

Thompson, A. G. (1991). The development of teachers' conceptions of mathematics teaching. In R. G. Underhill (Ed.), *Proceedings of the thirteenth annual meeting of the North American chapter of the International Group for the Psychology of Mathematics Education* (Vol. 2, pp. 8–14). Blacksburgh, VA: Virginia Polytechnic Institute.

Thompson, A. G. (1992). Teachers' beliefs and conceptions: A synthesis of the research. In D. Grouws (Ed.), *Handbook on research on teaching mathematics and learning* (pp. 127–146). New York: Macmillan.

Tobin, K. (1983). The influence of wait-time on classroom learning. *European Journal of Science Education, 5*(1), 35–48.

Van Manen, M. (1977). Linking ways of knowing with ways of being practical. *Curriculum Inquiry, 6,* 205–228.

Von Glasersfeld, E. (1987). Learning as a constructive activity. In C. Janvier (Ed.), *Problems of representation in the teaching and learning of mathematics* (pp. 3–17). Hillsdale, NJ: Lawrence Erlbaum Associates.

Von Glasersfeld, E. (1991). Abstraction, re-presentation, and reflection: An interpretation of experience and Piaget's approach. In L. P. Steffe (Ed.), *Epistemological foundations of mathematical experience* (pp. 45–67). New York: Springer-Verlag.

Vygotsky, L. S. (1978). *Mind in society: The development of higher psychological processes.* Cambridge, MA: Harvard University Press.

Wood, P., Bruner, J., & Ross, G. (1976). The role of tutoring in problem solving. *Journal of Child Psychology and Psychiatry, 17,* 89–100.

Wood, T., Cobb, P., & Yackel, E. (1995). Reflections on learning and teaching mathematics in elementary school. In L. Steffe & J. Gale (Eds.), *Constructivism in education* (pp. 401–422). Hillsdale, NJ: Lawrence Erlbaum Associates.

Zimmerman, B. J. (1990). Self-regulated learning and academic achievement. *Educational Psychologist, 25*(1), 3–17.

Author Index

Subject Index